The Niles Car
and Manufacturing Company

Engraving No. 359. "Single End" Interurban Combination Passenger and Baggage Car

Interurban and Suburban Motorcars, Trolley Cars & Passenger Cars

ISBN #978-1-935700-32-6

Engraving No. 501—42 Ft. Light Interurban, Three Compartment, Passenger, Smoking and Baggage Car.

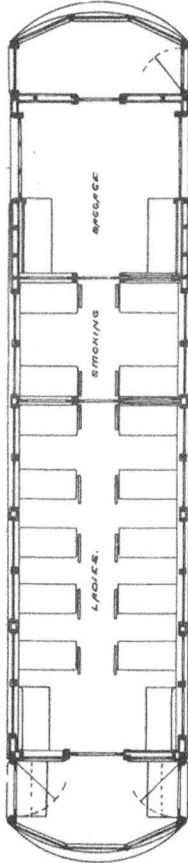

Drawing No. 501—Plan of 42 Ft. Three Compartment, Passenger, Smoking and Baggage Car.

42 FT. LIGHT INTERURBAN, COMBINATION PASSENGER, SMOKING AND BAGGAGE CAR

For single or double end service, designed especially for short interurban lines where the traffic is not heavy but first class accommodations, frequent schedule and baggage transportation are advisable on account of steam railroad competition.

Under usual conditions the car is run with baggage end in front and passenger entrances at each side of rear end. Where stops are made at "near side" of crossings, the passenger end is run forward, and where there are no facilities for turning cars at terminals, either end is run in front and passengers and baggage handled in front or rear. This plan is working very satisfactorily in actual service.

General Specifications and Dimensions

Length over buffers..................................... 42' 0"
Length over vestibules................................ 41' 0"
Length of car body..................................... 32' 6"
Length of main passenger compartment.... 17' 2¾"
Length of smoking compartment............... 5' 9⅝"
Length of baggage room............................. 5' 5⅝"
Length of rear vestibule............................. 4' 6"
Length of front vestibule........................... 4' 0"
Width over sheathing at sills..................... 8' 6"
Width over all (or to suit purchaser)........ 8' 8½"
Height, under sills to top of roof.............. 9' 4½"
Height, from track to top of roof.............. 12' 2½"
Distance between bolster centers............. 12' 8"
Wheel base of trucks.................................. 6' 1"
Seating capacity.. 38
Length of seats... 36½"
Width of aisle.. 20½"
Weight of car body, about........................ 18,000 lbs.
Weight of trucks.. 14,600 lbs.
Weight complete on track, including Allis-Chalmers No. 301 40 H. P. quadruple electric equipment and air brakes, about... 23 tons.

BOTTOM FRAME. Semi-steel under frame of two 6" I-beam center sills, two 7" channel side sills, two 9" steel plate truss bolsters, two 6" I needle beams, two 4" x 3" end sill angles, eight ½" reinforcing plates, two ½" x 7" buffer plates, two 1⅜" under truss rods, fourteen ¾" tie rods, and to which suitable wooden sills and cross framing are bolted.

FLOOR. Hard maple 1" thick, lengthwise of car, thoroughly painted and covered with hard wood strips in aisle and half oval iron at baggage doors.

BODY. Eight windows of Pullman twin style and one 4' 0" baggage door on each side. 30" sliding door in rear bulkhead. 24" sliding door in front bulkhead. Alternate single and panel side posts. Truss braced below windows and sheathed outside with narrow tongue and groove poplar.

ROOF. Monitor deck style. Concealed steel rafters. Covered with No. 8 duck thoroughly painted and fitted with trolley platform full length.

VESTIBULES. Flush with car floor, supported on steel center sills. Rear vestibule fitted with 30" swinging door, double steps with safety treads and Edwards' self-raising steel trap door on each side. Front vestibule has 24" swing door and iron stirrup steps on right side and window on left side, and is for employes only. Three drop sashes across each vestibule end.

INTERIOR FINISH. Selected mahogany with inlaid marquetry lines. Vaulted Empire ceiling in green and gold. Bronze trimmings. Eight rod bottom parcel racks.

SEATS. Main compartment has 8 Hale & Kilburn No. 199-EE steel seats with head-roll backs, bronze grab handles, automatic foot rests, spring edge cushions, aisle arm rests, upholstered with dark green plush; also four corner seats with stationary backs. Smoking room has four cross seats with stationary backs against bulkheads, upholstered with woven rattan. Baggage room has folding wooden seats.

HEATERS. Electric type, ten Consolidated No. 203-S truss plank style.

WINDOWS AND GLASS. All main window and partition sashes glazed with selected double strength car glass; all doors (except baggage) with ¼" plate glass. Gothic sashes with seven pieces of cathedral glass in zinc channels. Five large movable deck sashes on each side, hung on Hart's ratchets and glazed with tinted art glass. Pantasote curtains with Forsyth No. 88 fixtures. Side sashes fitted with Edwards' locks with concealed racks.

GRAB HANDLES. Hickory in malleable iron sockets on each side of door; also diagonal handles on rear vestibule door.

LIGHTING. Wire, switches, fuses and sockets for twenty 16 c. p. lamps on separate bases, also concealed portion of trolley power cable, are supplied and installed by Car Builder.

DRAW BARS AND COUPLERS. Each end of car fitted with radial draw bar with Niles standard coupler.

SANDERS. One compressed air sander on each end of car.

PILOTS. One locomotive style cut out for radial draw bar, on each end of car.

HEADLIGHT. Supplied by Purchaser, wiring and brackets on each end by Car Builder.

TROLLEY RETRIEVER. One Wilson type on each end of car.

MISCELLANEOUS FITTINGS. Two alarm gongs, two signal bells, four brackets for tail lamps, emergency tools, advertising mouldings, and two illuminated signs, are supplied by Car Builder.

PAINTING. Color, lettering, numbers and striping as directed by Purchaser.

HAND BRAKES. Lindstrom malleable iron ratchet lever on each end of car.

AIR BRAKES. Supplied by Purchaser and may be installed by Car Builder at extra charge for same.

ELECTRIC POWER EQUIPMENT. Supplied by Purchaser and may be installed by Car Builder at extra charge for same.

TRUCKS. Baldwin Class 72-18-S with Standard 33" forged-rolled steel wheels 3½" treads, fitted on 5" hammered steel axles with 4¼" x 8" journals, and prepared for Allis-Chalmers 40 H. P. motors, (or motors specified by Purchaser) are supplied by Car Builder. If cars can be delivered on track on their own wheels, the bodies should be mounted on trucks at Car Works; otherwise by Purchaser at destination.

Detail specifications and drawings are submitted for Purchaser's approval before starting work.

Prices can be quoted on duplicates of car as specified above, or with any exceptions desired.

Engraving No. 480—51 Ft. "Double End" Special Parlor Car with Smoking Room and Lavatory.

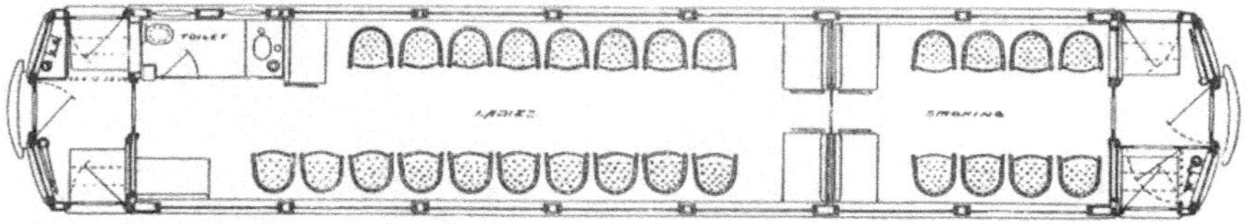

Drawing No. 480—Plan of 51 Ft. "Double End" Special Parlor Car with Smoking Room, Toilet and Lavatory.

Engraving No. 480—Interior of 51 Ft. Special Parlor Car.

51 FT. DOUBLE END, SPECIAL PARLOR CAR WITH SMOKING ROOM AND LAVATORY

For chartering to private parties, excursions, special purposes and extra fare service. It is richly finished, has large observation windows fitted with spring balances, carpeted floor and movable parlor chairs, yet the cost is not excessive and it can be quickly converted for regular traffic by removing the chairs and carpet and substituting regular reversible back car seats.

It is arranged for running with either end forward; therefore, can be held on sidings for theater and special parties, and started in either direction.

General Specifications and Dimensions

Length over buffers	51' 0"
Length over vestibules	49' 4"
Length of main passenger compartment	28' 9½"
Length of smoking compartment	12' 1"
Length of vestibules	4' 2"
Width over sheathing at sills	8' 6½"
Width over all (or to suit Purchaser)	8' 9"
Height, under sills to top of roof	9' 4½"
Height, from track to top of roof	12' 9½"
Distance between bolster centers	29' 0"
Wheel base of trucks	6' 6"
Seating capacity, 26 parlor chairs, or 52 persons when fitted with coach seats.	
Length of coach seats	37"
Width of aisle when used as regular coach	19½"
Weight of car body, about	29,000 lbs.
Weight of trucks	20,322 lbs.
Weight complete on track, including G. E. No. 205-1200 volt D. C. 75 H. P. 4 motor electric equipment and automatic air brakes, about	39 tons

Bottom Frame. Semi-steel under frame composed of four 6" steel I-beams in center and intermediate sills extending full length under vestibules to buffers, two ⅝" x 7¾" steel plates (8" channels at Purchasers option) in side sills, two ½" x 6" end sill plates, two 6" I needle beams, two 10" steel plate truss bolsters, ¾" tie rod with turn buckle in center at each cross sill, and two 1⅝" under truss rods with 1¾" turnbuckles. (Riveted all steel under frame can be supplied with this car.)

Floor. Double thickness, 1⅛" x 3¼" yellow pine with water-proof tar felt between and covered with Greenwich inlaid linoleum. Floor is carpeted by Purchaser when used as a parlor car.

Body. Seven wide, large sash single windows with semi-elliptical tops and panels between on each side of car. Truss braced below windows, ½" vertical tie rod in each post, ½" x 2" inside truss bars and sheathed outside with ¾" x 2" poplar.

Roof. Monitor deck style extending over each vestibule; ½" x 1½" concealed steel rafter at each panel post; covered with No. 8 canvas thoroughly painted and fitted with trolley platform over each truck supported over deck sills.

Vestibules. At each end, flush with car floor, supported on main sills of car. 27" swing door with triple steps having ¼" steel plate hangers, safety treads and Edwards' self-raising steel trap door at each side. 27" swing door with drop sash and three bevel locks in center of each vestibule end. Convertible motorman's cab at curb side of front end with upper half of outside door to swing separate from lower half. At rear end the controlling apparatus is enclosed and passengers admitted on both sides.

Interior Finish. Selected mahogany in large smooth panels with inlaid borders. Window heads with same curvature as on outside. Double Gothic sashes between which the lower sashes raise. Pantasote curtains with Forsyth fixtures in mahogany casings below Gothic sashes. Full Empire ceiling in green and gold. Bronze trimmings. Thirteen rod bottom parcel racks.

Furniture, Carpet and Draperies. Loose parlor chairs, removable carpets, additional window draperies, linen and any extra fittings are selected and supplied by Purchaser, or may be supplied by Car Builder at extra cost of same. Car Builder supplies permanent fittings, viz.: linoleum floor covering, pantasote curtains, and a complete set of leather upholstered coach seats as specified.

Toilet and Lavatory. Occupies the length of two side windows and is fitted with bronze oval sash with ventilator, water flush hopper, nickeline washstand with locker beneath, bevel edge mirror, comb, brush and towel racks, overhead water tank with necessary pipe, fittings, etc., cement floor, ventilator in roof and water cooler.

Seats. Twenty Hale & Kilburn No. 199-EE steel seats with reversible head-roll backs, bronze grab handles, automatic foot rests, spring edge cushions, mahogany aisle arm rests and upholstered in dark green leather, and six seats with stationary backs, are supplied and installed by Car Builder if the car is intended for both regular coach and parlor car service. If for special service exclusively, these seats are omitted and their value credited to Purchaser, who selects and supplies parlor furniture instead.

Heater. Electric style supplied and installed by Purchaser, or by Car Builder as specified by Purchaser at extra cost of same.

Windows and Glass. Lower side sashes hung on Edwards' spring balances and glazed with polished plate glass 53¾" x 24". Outside Gothic sashes glazed each with seven pieces cathedral glass in zinc channels. Inside Gothic sashes have leaded art glass in metal frames. Deck windows have fourteen large sashes in centers, hinged at ends, operated by separate bronze handles and small stationary sashes at each side, all glazed with tinted cathedral glass. All doors, partitions and vestibule sashes glazed with heavy plate glass.

Grab Handles. Hickory in malleable iron sockets on each side of each vestibule side door; also diagonal handles on outside of doors.

Window Guards. Removable four rod painted iron guards on side windows; inside guards of bronze.

Lighting. Conduits, condulets, wire, switches, fuses, sockets, brackets and frosted shades for 32—16 c. p. lamps on separate bases, are supplied and installed by Car Builder.

Draw Bars and Couplers. Janney automatic M. C. B. radial type with radial spring buffers for 50' radius curve, on each end of car.

Track Sanders. One compressed air sander on each end of car with flexible connections to pipes attached to trucks to place sand under each leading wheel.

Fenders. Special design supplied and attached by Purchaser, or may be supplied by Car Builder at extra charge for same.

Headlight. One combination arc and incandescent with brackets and wiring on each end of car.

Trolley Retrievers. Supplied and attached by Purchaser, or by Car Builder at extra cost of same.

Fare Register. Supplied by Purchaser. Square rod with leather pulls along one side of roof supplied and attached by Car Builder.

Miscellaneous Fittings. Two alarm gongs, two signal bells with fittings, four red signal lens, four tail lamp brackets, emergency tools, switch iron, switch cabinets and six sets of Automatic ventilators, are supplied by Car Builder.

Painting. Color, lettering, numbers and striping as directed by Purchaser.

Hand Brakes. Lindstrom malleable iron ratchet lever on each end of car.

Air Brakes. Supplied by Purchaser and may be installed by Car Builder at extra charge for same.

Electric Power Equipment. Supplied and installed by Purchaser at destination, or may be installed by Car Builder at extra charge for same. Concealed portion of trolley cable only may be supplied and installed by Car Builder at extra cost of same.

Trucks. Baldwin Class 78-25-A with Standard 36" forged-rolled steel wheels having 3" treads, fitted on 5½" hammered steel axles with 4¼" x 8" journals and prepared for 4 G. E. No. 205-1200 V. D. C. 75 H. P. motors (or as specified by Purchaser), are supplied by Car Builder. If cars can be delivered on track on their own wheels the bodies should be mounted on trucks at Car Works; otherwise by Purchaser at destination.

Engraving No. 428—"Double End" Interurban Trailer Coach

Engraving No. 427—"Single End" Combination Passenger and Baggage Motor Car

TRAIN OF 58 FT. COMBINATION PASSENGER AND BAGGAGE MOTOR CAR WITH PASSENGER TRAILER CAR

For electric railways constructed and operated according to steam railroad practice.

They are of standard steam coach width, fitted with automatic M. C. B. radial couplers with spring buffers and continuous train passageway and can be run in train over 50 foot radius city curves.

The trailer car is attached only when traffic warrants, for excursions, chartering to special parties, laying over at intermediate points and other service for which the use of a separate motor car would not be convenient nor economical.

One conductor has charge of both cars, the train passageway being used between stations but the end doors are locked when on city streets and short curves.

The trailer car has a lighting trolley and hot water heater for keeping it light and warm when waiting at terminals and sidings and all outside doors lock with key.

All side windows are fitted with double sashes, the lower ones raising between the Gothic sashes and the curtains ɔvering the lower sashes only.

General Specifications of Combination Motor Car

Length over buffers	58' 6¼"	Height, track to top of roof	13' 0¾"
Length over vestibules	56' 11¾"	Distance between bolster centers	35' 6"
Length of baggage compartment	11' 10¾"	Wheel base of trucks	7' 0"
Length of smoking compartment	11' 2¼"	Seating capacity	54
Length of main passenger compartment	29' 5⅝"	Length of seats	40½"
Length of rear vestibule	4' 4½"	Width of aisle	22½"
Width at sills, including panels	9' 7½"	Weight of car body	37,000 lbs.
Width over all	9' 10"	Weight of trucks	23,000 lbs.
Height, under sills to top of roof	9' 6¾"		

Bottom Frame. Two outside sills of yellow pine, double, with ⅝" x 7¾" steel plates between; four intermediate sills of 6" steel I-beams.

Trusses. 1⅝" under truss rods on 8" needle I-beams; ½" x 2" inside truss bars.

Floor. Double with waterproof building felt between and covered in aisles with 24" corrugated rubber mat.

Body. Twin Pullman style windows with double sashes and panel posts framed and sheathed similar to steam coaches.

Motorman's Cab. In right-hand front corner with door in each side and solid panel at rear.

Baggage Room. At front end with 42" sliding door in each side.

Rear Vestibule. With triple steps having Empire treads, 31" swinging door and trap doors on each side, and 27" swinging door in end.

Train Passage and Buffers. At rear end, supported at top and bottom on four spring plungers. Plaited diaphragm connects chafing plates and door posts. Buffers are beveled at ends so as to automatically compress when on tangent and form closed passage between cars. The end doors are kept locked when on city streets with short curves and the passage used only when on interurban track with long radius curves.

Roof. With steel rafter at each panel post, covered with 8 oz. canvas, painted and fitted with trolley platform.

Windows. Double lower sashes fitted with Edwards' fixtures, to raise between stationary double Gothic sashes.

Glass. Selected D. T. A. car glass in lower windows; cathedral glass in Gothic and deck sashes; heavy plate glass in doors.

Curtains. Pantasote on spring rollers below the Gothic sashes.

Interior Finish. Selected mahogany in passenger compartment with Empire ceiling; dark English oak in smoking room with paneled ceiling; 12 bronze parcel racks and bronze trimmings.

Toilet Room. With water flush closet, cement floor, white enamel finish and water cooler in alcove on outside.

Seats. Hale & Kilburn No. 99-EE style, of plush in passenger room and rattan in smoker, as located in drawing.

Grab Handles. Hickory, in malleable iron sockets at each side of doors and diagonal handle on each vestibule door.

Window Guards. Of bronze, on end windows only.

Lighting. Wiring and separate bases for 40 lamps, one over each seat on side posts, and concealed portion of trolley cable, supplied by Car Builder.

Draw Bars and Couplers. Janney automatic M. C. B. radial, with radial spring buffers.

Track Sanders. Two Nichols-Lintern air style, on front end.

Pilot. Locomotive style, under front end.

Trolley Retriever. One Knutson No. 2, at rear end of car.

Heater. Smith No. 1 hot water style, located in baggage room.

Hand Brakes. Malleable iron Lindstrom brake at front end.

Miscellaneous Fittings. Signal bells, alarm gong, switch iron, emergency tools, air signal, are supplied by Car Builder. Fare register, headlight and rear lights are supplied by Purchaser.

Air Brakes. Westinghouse automatic single end type, supplied by Purchaser and installed by Car Builder.

Electric Power Equipment. Supplied and installed by Purchaser at destination.

Trucks. Baldwin Class 84-30-A with Standard 36" M. C. B. section rolled steel wheels on 6" hammered steel axles with 5" x 9" journals; built for 4 Westinghouse No. 112-B 75 H. P. motors and speed of 65 m. p. h. are fitted to car body and delivered on steam railroad track ready for transportation on own wheels. Unless cars can be delivered on their own wheels the bodies should be mounted on trucks by Purchaser at destination.

If price is wanted on this car, state that it is to be as specified above or name exceptions desired.

Detail drawings and specifications are submitted for Purchaser's approval before starting work.

General Specifications of Passenger Trailer Car

This car is of the same style and finish as the combination car, except as follows:

Length over buffers	58' 9"
Length over vestibules	57' 1"
Length of body	48' 2½"

Train passage and buffers at each end.

Vestibule and steps at each end.

Men's and women's toilets (2) in diagonal opposite corners.

Heater and removable corner seat opposite one toilet.

Single passenger compartment without smoker, baggage room or motorman's cab; finished same as passenger compartment of combination car.

No track sanders, alarm gong, switch iron, trolley retriever or pilot are supplied with trailer car.

A trolley for lighting current only at one end of car.

Air brakes are Westinghouse automatic trailer type with couplings at each end.

Hand brake and electric couplings at each end of car.

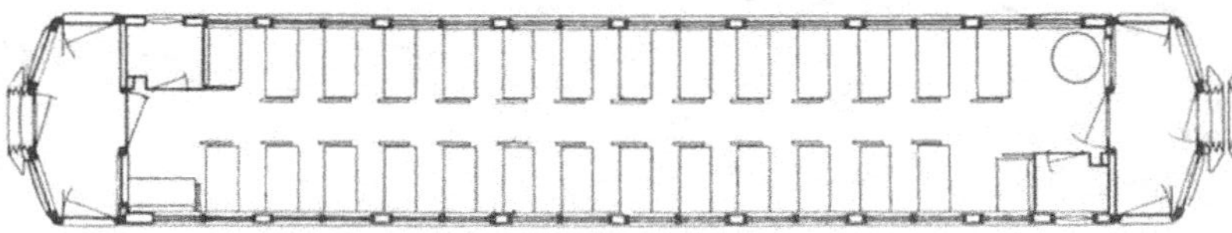

Drawing No. 428—Plan of "Double End" Trailer Coach

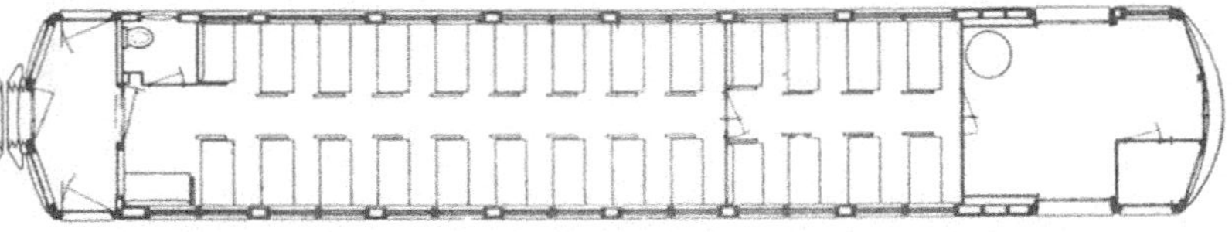

Drawing No. 427—Plan of "Single End" Combination Motor Car

Engraving No. 418—"Single End" Interurban Passenger Car

56 FT. "SINGLE END" INTERURBAN PASSENGER CAR

For limited service on long runs and at fast speed. They are for use singly only, therefore, do not have end doors nor automatic couplers.

They are equipped with four 90 H. P. motors, 37" steel wheels and make 60 miles per hour in regular service.

General Specifications and Dimensions

Length over buffers	56' 1½"	Height, under sills to top of roof	9' 5"
Length over vestibules	55' 1½"	Height, track to top of roof	12' 11"
Length of car body	45' 8⅜"	Distance between bolster centers	33' 9"
Length of front vestibule	5' 5¾"	Wheel base of trucks	7' 0"
Length of rear vestibule	3' 11¾"	Seating capacity	62
Length of main passenger compartment	31' 2"	Length of seats	36¾"
Length of smoking compartment	14' 6½"	Width of aisles	19"
Width over sheathing at sills	8' 5½"	Weight of car body	30,500 lbs.
Width over all	8' 8"	Weight of trucks	21,520 lbs.

BOTTOM FRAME. Two outside sills of 5" x 8" and 2" x 6" yellow pine with 6" steel channel bolted between. Two center and two intermediate sills of 6" steel I-beams filled with yellow pine and extending under vestibules from buffer to buffer. The six steel sills are supported on and bolted to six transverse steel beams, viz, two 8" needle I-beams, two 10" bolsters and two 7" x 7" T-beams under end sills; ¾" tie rods with turnbuckles in center at each cross sill.

TRUSSES. Two 1½" diameter under truss rods with 1¾" turnbuckles and two ⅜" x 2½" inside truss bars on pedestals over bolsters for supporting overhanging ends.

FLOOR. Double thickness of ⅞" x 3¼" yellow pine with waterproof building felt between, and covered with Greenwich inlaid linoleum.

BODY. Pullman style double Gothic windows with alternate single and panel posts, braced and sheathed on outside with ¾" x 2" poplar, continuous from sills to letter panel between windows.

ROOF. Monitor deck style with steam coach hoods; concealed steel rafter at each panel post. Covered with No. 6 Canvas and fitted with trolley platform at rear end.

VESTIBULES. At front end for motorman only, with swing door and stirrup steps at right side; at rear end with 30" swing door and triple steps covered with trap doors on each side.

SMOKING ROOM. At front end, including five side windows and with swing door in each end.

TOILET ROOM. In left-hand rear corner, with Duner closet, cement floor, white enamel finish, and water cooler in alcove on outside.

WINDOWS. Twin Pullman style with single lower sashes, fitted with Edwards' double lock fixtures to raise between double Gothic sashes. Deck sashes in three sections; the center ones hinged at one end and operated by bronze openers.

DOORS. 30" sliding door in rear body bulkhead. All other doors of swing style as shown in drawing.

GLASS. Polished plate in lower side and end windows, partitions and doors; rippled opalescent glass in deck and outside Gothic sashes; leaded art glass in inside Gothic sashes.

CURTAINS. Pantasote, on spring rollers in casings below the Gothic sashes.

INTERIOR FINISH. Selected burl mahogany in wide, smooth panels with marquetry borders. Window heads of same curvature as on outside. Statuary bronze trimmings and sectional rod bottom parcel racks.

SEATS. Hale & Kilburn's No. 110-C-E steel type with grab handle and spring edge, upholstered with figured green plush in main compartment and leather in smoking room.

GRAB HANDLES. Pullman style of solid bronze on each side of each outside door.

WINDOW GUARDS. Four-rod painted iron sectional guards on side windows, hinged at top for cleaning glass.

LIGHTING. Wire, switches, fuses, lamp brackets and concealed part of trolley cable, are supplied and installed by Car Builder. Separate base for each lamp located along deck sills and panel posts.

DRAW BARS AND COUPLERS. Each buffer is fitted with a large cast steel rigid draw head and a coupling bar 1½" x 3" x 5' is carried on hooks under side of car.

TRACK SANDERS. Two Nichols-Lintern air type on front end of car.

FENDER. One Providence interurban fender on front end.

HEADLIGHT. One 16" Mosher arc style on front end of car.

TROLLEY RETRIEVER. One Knutson No. 2 on rear end of car.

HEATER. One Smith No. 2-C hot water style in front vestibule with pipes and foot guards along each side.

HAND BRAKES. In front vestibule, vertical geared 14" iron wheel with Peacock C drum

REGISTER ROD. With leather pulls along one side of car.

MISCELLANEOUS FITTINGS. Signal bells, alarm gong, switch iron, roof steps, mats and handles, coal box, advertising mouldings, illuminated dash sign and sign and flag box, are supplied by Car Builder.

AIR BRAKES. Supplied by Purchaser and may be installed by Car Builder at shop cost plus 10%.

ELECTRIC POWER EQUIPMENT. Supplied and installed by Purchaser at destination, or may be installed by Car Builder at shop cost plus 10%.

TRUCKS. Baldwin Class 84-30-A with Standard 37" rolled steel wheels having 4³⁄₁₆" x 3" rims, on 6" hammered steel axles with 5" x 9" journals, and prepared for Westinghouse No. 112-B motors, are supplied by Car Builder. If cars can be delivered on track on their own wheels, it is advisable to have trucks fitted to cars at car works, otherwise by Purchaser at destination.

Prices can be quoted on duplicates of car as specified above, or state exceptions desired.

Detail specifications and drawings are submitted for Purchaser's approval before starting work.

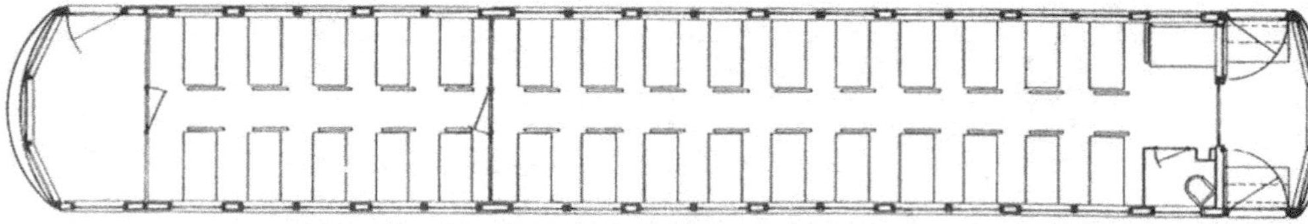

Drawing No. 418—Plan of "Single End" Interurban Passenger Car

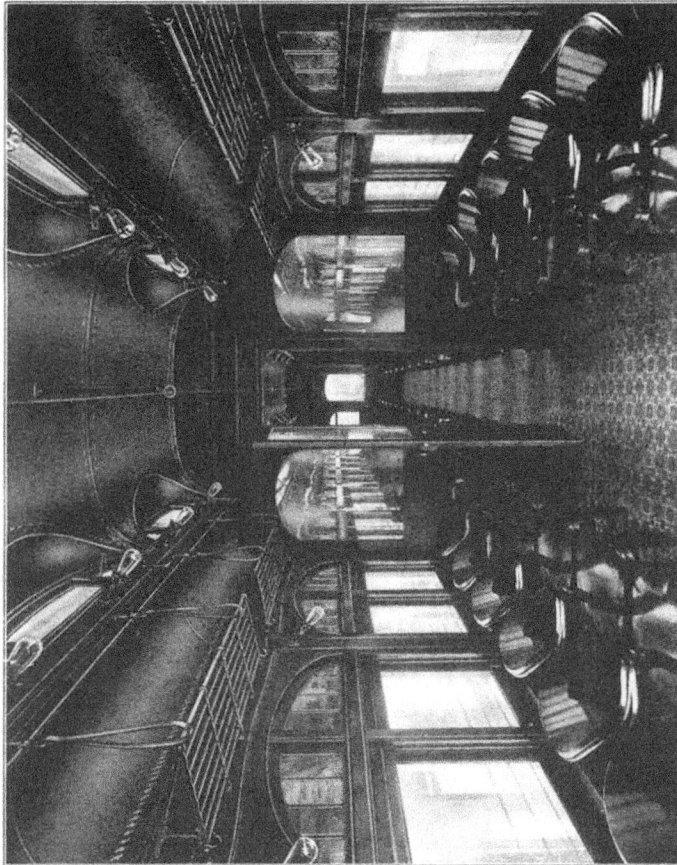

Interior of "Single End" Semi-Parlor Car and Passenger Car

56 FT. "SINGLE END" SEMI-PARLOR INTERURBAN CAR

For chartering to parties, special use of railway officials and for regular limited service when urgently needed.

It is similar to the limited coach shown on opposite page, except as follows:

Toilet. Occupies the length of two windows and is fitted with nickeline washstand with closet beneath, tank, mirror, comb and brush rack, etc.

Seats. In forward or parlor compartment are twelve movable solid mahogany chairs with leather buffers and upholstering, selected and supplied by the Purchaser, but these chairs may be supplied by the Car Builder at extra cost of same.

The main passenger compartment has Hale & Kilburn's No. 199-EE seats with reversible backs, bronze grab handles, spring edge cushions and covered with figured green plush, and are supplied by Car Builder.

6

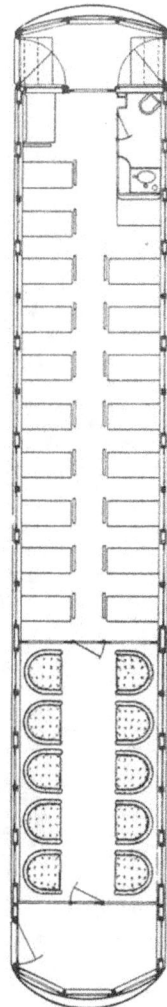

Drawing No. 418-A—Plan of "Single End" Semi-Parlor Interurban Car

Engraving No. 384—"Double End" Single Compartment Trailer Coach

58 FT. SINGLE COMPARTMENT COACH

For train service either as motor or trailer car, for long runs and fast speed, and for varying traffic which demands changes in lengths of trains on short notice.

The car illustrated is used as a trailer, but is fitted with multiple unit control and bus lines, train pipes, couplings and end doors, so it can be used between motor cars or at ends of trains. They were pulled in steam railroad trains from Niles Car Works to the Pacific Coast.

General Specifications and Dimensions

Length over buffers	57' 8"	Distance between bolster centers	36' 3"
Length over vestibules	56' 4"	Wheel base of trucks	6' 6"
Length of body	47' 3½"	Seating capacity	62
Length of vestibules	4' 6"	Length of seats	40"
Width at sills, including sheathing	9' 1½"	Width of aisle	20"
Width over all	9' 4"	Weight of car body	34,600 lbs.
Height, under sills to top of roof	9' 6½"	Weight of trucks	21,460 lbs.
Height, track to top of roof	12' 10"		

Bottom Frame. Two outside sills of 4½" x 7¾" and 1⅞" x 6" yellow pine with ⅝" x 7¾" steel plate bolted between. Four center and intermediate sills of 6" steel I-beams extending under vestibules from buffer to buffer. All six sills are supported on and bolted to six transverse steel beams, viz., two 8" needle I-beams, two 10" plate bolsters and two 5" x 3½" angles under end sills; ¾" tie rods with turnbuckles in center at each cross sill.

Trusses. Two under truss rods 1½" diameter; two inside truss bars ½" x 2" for supporting overhanging ends.

Floor. Double thickness with waterproof building felt between and hard wood aisle strips between seats.

Body. Eight pairs of Pullman style twin windows with alternate single and panel posts. Sheathed outside with ¾" x 2" poplar

Roof. Monitor deck with steam coach hoods; concealed steel rafter at each panel post; covered with No. 8 cotton duck and fitted with trolley plank full length.

Vestibules. At each end, with 31" swing door, triple steps with bronze binding, Empire treads and trap doors on each side, and 27" doors in ends.

Interior Finish. Single passenger compartment with one toilet, of selected mahogany with curved window heads and mouldings and main panels with inlaid borders of marquetry lines. Empire ceiling of five-ply veneer, painted and decorated, bronze trimmings and sectional parcel racks.

Toilet Room. With dry hopper, cement floor, white enamel finish and water cooler in alcove on outside.

Windows. Twin Gothic style, sashes fitted with Edwards' fixtures and Pantasote curtains on spring rollers. Deck sashes on Hart's ratchets.

Doors. All of swing type, 1½" thick; 31" doors in end bulkheads.

Glass. Polished plate in doors; D. T. A. selected car glass in lower windows and bulkheads; opalescent art glass in zinc channels in Gothic sashes and small panes in decks.

Seats. Heywood Bros. & Wakefield Co.'s No. 54-A-G-F type with bronze handle, spring edge, aisle arm rest, pedestal base and upholstered with green plush.

Grab Handles. Hickory, in bronze sockets at each side of steps; also diagonal handle on each vestibule door. Malleable iron handles at end doors and on roof.

Lighting. Wire, brackets, sockets, switches and fuses for 35 lamps and concealed portion of trolley cable are supplied and installed by Car Builder. Separate bases for all lamps, located along deck sills and eight lamps with holophane shades along center of ceiling.

Draw Bars and Couplers. Automatic M. C. B. radial, with Janney couplers.

Pilots. One locomotive style under each end, located to allow coupling to other cars.

Heaters. Twelve Consolidated truss plank style electric heaters per car, complete with switches, fuses and wire.

Hand Brakes. Malleable iron Lindstrom lever in each vestibule.

Miscellaneous Fittings. Signal bells, emergency tools, air signals, wiring for headlight, brackets for signal lamps, roof steps, mats and handles, are supplied by Car Builder.

Control Line. Of seven-wire cable in steel conduits with junction boxes and two control sockets at each end of car and one control jumper cable, supplied and installed by Car Builder.

Bus Line. In steel conduit with coupler socket at each end of car for G. E. No. 73 quadruple motor equipment. Lighting and heat circuits are taken from bus line. Supplied and installed by Car Builder.

Air Brakes. Westinghouse A. M. R. double end trailer car equipment with R-2 triple valve and conductor's valve under corner seat with red cord along deck sill to end of each vestibule, are supplied by Purchaser and installed by Car Builder.

Electric Power Equipment. Supplied and installed by Purchaser at destination.

Trucks. Baldwin Class 78-30-B with Standard 36" M. C. B. section rolled steel wheels on 5½" hammered steel axles with 4¼" x 8" journals and prepared for G. E. No. 73 motors, are supplied and attached to car body by Car Builder and delivered on track ready for transportation on own wheels to destination in steam railroad trains. If cars cannot be delivered on own wheels, the trucks should be attached to car bodies by Purchaser at destination.

If price is wanted on this car, state that it is to be as specified above or name exceptions desired.

Detail specifications and drawings are submitted for Purchaser's approval before starting work.

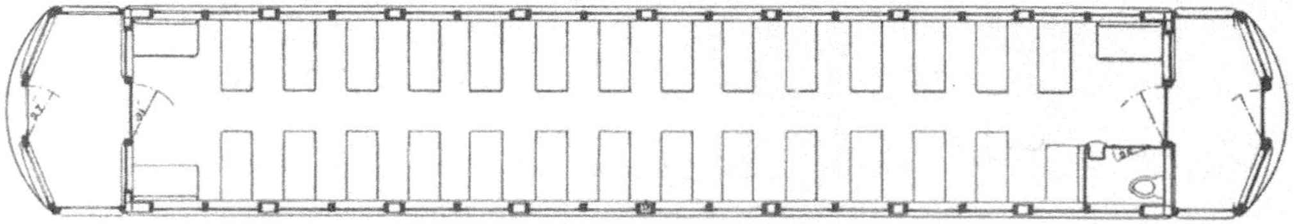

Drawing No. 384—Plan of "Double End" Single Compartment Trailer Coach

56 FT. STEEL UNDERFRAME, SINGLE COMPARTMENT TRAILER COACH

For train service and long distance, high speed interurban traffic in which it is important that the service be equal to or better than competing steam lines. This car is so arranged that it may be quickly equipped for motor service when so desired and is especially designed to withstand a hot dry climate for long periods and for the comfort of passengers.

General Specifications and Dimensions

Length over buffers	56' 0"	Distance between bolster centers	34' 6¾"
Length over vestibules	55' 2"	Wheel base of trucks	6' 6"
Length over end sills	45' 6"	Seating capacity	64
Length of vestibules	4' 10"	Length of seats	37"
Width over sheathing at sills	8' 9¾"	Width of aisle	21¼"
Width over all	9' 0"	Weight of car body, about	30,000 lbs.
Width inside	7' 11¼"	Weight of trucks (motor)	20,500 lbs.
Height, under sills to top of roof	9' 7"	Total weight on track equipped as trailer, about	27 tons
Height, from track to top of roof	13' 0"		

Engraving No. 498—56 Ft. Steel Underframe, Single Compartment Trailer Coach.

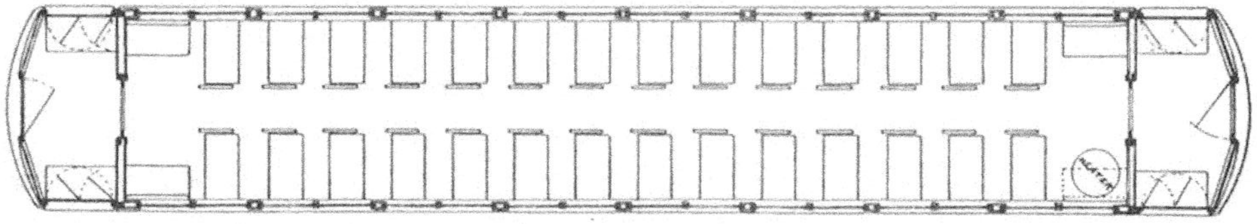

Drawing No. 498—Plan of 56 Ft. One Compartment Trailer Coach with Hot Water Heater.

Bottom Frame. An all steel under frame is riveted together before any wooden parts are bolted to same and consists of two center sills of 8"—18 lb. I beams, two side sills of 8"—13¾ lb. channels, two intermediate or platform sills at each end of 6"—10½ lb. channels extending from buffers to first cross sills beyond bolsters, two buffers of 8"—18¾ lb. channels, two end sills of 6" 10½ lb. channels with 5"—9 lb. channels riveted on top with flanges upward, twelve cross sills of 6"—10½ lb. channels and six cross sille of 5"—9 lb. channels, all riveted together with two steel angles at each joint. Yellow pine side sills 4½" x 8" are bolted to outside of steel under frame. Wooden sills for floor and under ceiling are bolted to all steel cross sills and end sills. Oak buffers 2¾" thick are secured to 2½" x 3½" steel angles riveted to all longitudinal steel sills. Bottom frame is supported on two 10" steel plate truss bolsters with riveted steel channel fillers and two 8"—18 lb. I needle beams on two 1½" truss rods with 1¾" turnbuckles.

Floor. One thickness of 13/16" x 3¼" yellow pine laid diagonal and one thickness of 13/16" x 3¼" hard maple laid lengthwise of car with waterproof tar felt between. The bottom is ceiled 1½" beneath the under floor and this space packed with mineral wool. All flooring is thoroughly painted on both sides and edges before laid. Corrugated rubber mat 24" wide full length of aisle.

Body. Eight pairs of Pullman style twin windows on each side with alternate single and panel posts; sheathed outside with ¾" x 2" poplar; inside truss bars ⅜" x 2", thoroughly braced beneath windows and with ⅝" vertical tie rod at each post; 30" sliding door in each end bulkhead.

Roof. Monitor deck type, extending over vestibules, with ⅜" x 1½" concealed steel rafters; 9/16" cypress roofing covered with No. 8 duck laid in white lead, copper flashing and thoroughly painted.

Vestibules. Each end has enclosed vestibule with 34" double folding door, triple steps with malleable iron hangers, wooden treads covered with knob rubber and brass bindings, and Edwards' self-raising steel trap door on each side. Entire vestibule floor is covered with knob rubber. Swinging door for train passage in center of each vestibule end.

Interior Finish. Solid mahogany with double Gothic sashes; window heads with same curvature as on outside; main panels with inlaid borders of colored woods. Full Empire ceiling of agasote painted green with gold decorations, and broad mahogany inlaid panels separating vaulted sections. Trimmings of polished bronze; 14 rod bottom parcel racks.

Seats. 28 Hale & Kilburn's No. 199-EE steel slats with reversible backs, bronze grab handles, upholstered with dark green leather, spring edge cushions, automatic foot rests, and mahogany aisle arm rests; also 4 longitudinal corner seats with stationary backs One corner seat removable for heater in winter.

Heater. Smith No. 1-C hot water type occupying the space of one corner seat and removable in summer.

Windows. Lower side sashes fitted with Edwards' bevel lock and ratchet on each side with spring rollers at top and weather strips at top and bottom. Single drop sashes in vestibule end windows. Pantasote curtains with Forsyth No. 88 fixtures in casings below Gothic sashes. Double Gothic sashes between which the lower sashes raise. Twin deck sashes semi-elliptical in shape hung on Hart's ratchet fixtures. End doors to have drop sashes in upper portions.

Glass. ¼" plate glass in all doors and vestibule end sashes; leaded cathedral glass in Gothic and deck sashes; selected D. S. A. car glass in lower side windows.

Grab Handles. 1⅛" bronze tubes in bronze sockets on each side of each vestibule side door; also on outside of vestibule end windows.

Lighting. Wire, conduits, couplings, switches, fuses, sockets and lamp brackets for 60—16 c. p. lamps on separate bases, are supplied and installed by Car Builder.

Draw Bars and Couplers. Each end of car fitted with automatic M. C. B. radial draw bar and coupler, with air and electric couplings attached.

Engraving No. 498—Interior of 56 Ft. Trailer Coach.

Miscellaneous Fittings. Emergency tools in glass case, one Mitchell dry chemical fire extinguisher, corner brackets for signal lamps, 2 conductor's bells and fittings and vestibule window guards, are supplied and installed by Car Builder.

Painting. Color, lettering, numbers and striping as directed by Purchaser.

Hand Brakes. Supplied by Purchaser and may be installed by Car Builder at extra charge for same.

Electric Power Equipment. Train cable and power wiring supplied by Purchaser and may be installed by Car Builder at extra charge for same.

Trucks. Baldwin Class 78-30-A with Standard 36" M. C. B. section forged-rolled steel wheels on 5½" hammered steel axles with 5" x 9" journals and prepared for any motors specified by Purchaser so cars may be used for motor service when desired, are supplied by Car Builder. If cars can be delivered on track on their own wheels, the bodies should be mounted on trucks at Car Works; otherwise by Purchaser at destination.

Prices can be quoted on duplicates of car as specified above, or with any exceptions desired. Detail specifications and drawings are submitted for Purchaser's approval before starting work.

Engraving No. 458—58 Ft. "Single End" Smoking and Express, Mail and Baggage Car.

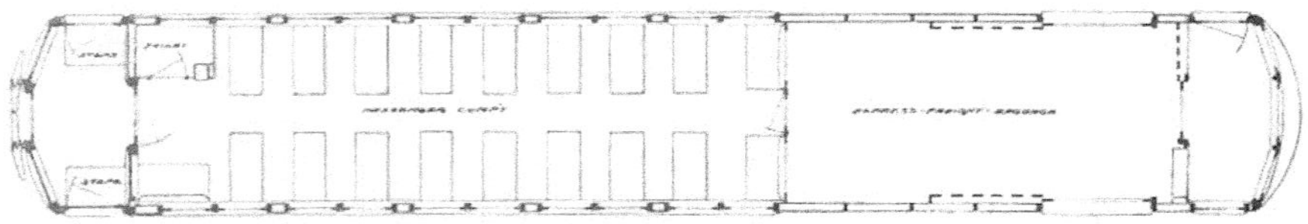

Drawing No. 458—Plan of 58 Ft. Two Compartment, Smoking and Express Car.

58 FT. SINGLE END COMBINATION SMOKING AND BAGGAGE, MAIL OR EXPRESS INTERURBAN MOTOR CAR

When used singly the rear compartment is for mixed passengers and smoking may be allowed in the baggage room. When run at front end of trains, which include regular coaches, the passenger compartment is used by smokers and the forward room for baggage, express or mail.

All doors of the baggage room can be locked on the inside. The motorman has separate compartment with side door. The rear end is fitted with spring buffers and diaphragm which form closed train passage when coupled to cars similarly equipped. This car is most suitable to traffic under practically steam road conditions.

General Specifications and Dimensions

Length over buffers	57′ 8″	Distance between bolster centers	36′ 3″
Length over vestibules	56′ 4″	Wheel base of trucks	6′ 6″
Length of passenger compartment	29′ 0″	Seating capacity	38
Length of baggage room	17′ 8″	Length of seats	40″
Length of vestibules	4′ 7¼″	Width of aisle	22″
Width over sheathing at sills	9′ 1½″	Weight of car body, about	34,000 lbs.
Width over all (or to suit Purchaser)	9′ 4″	Weight of trucks	21,460 lbs.
Width inside	8′ 4″	Weight complete on track including quadruple G. E. No. 73—75 H. P. single end control equipment and automatic air brakes, about	38½ tons
Height under sills to top of roof	9′ 6½″		
Height from track to top of roof	13′ 1″		

Bottom Frame. Semi-steel type: two outside sills composed of 4½″ x 7¾″ and 1¾″ x 6″ yellow pine with ⅝″ x 7¾″ steel plate (8″ steel channel at Purchaser's option) bolted between. Four center and intermediate sills of 6″ steel I beams, 10″ steel plate bolsters with riveted steel channel fillers, 8″ steel I needle beams, 20 tie rods ¾″ with turnbuckles in center, 1⅜″ under truss rods with 1¾″ turnbuckles. (Riveted all steel underframe can be supplied with this car.)

Floor. Double thickness 1⅜″ x 3¼″ yellow pine with ½″ Keystone Hair Insulator between.

Body. Pullman twin window style with alternate single and panel posts of oak, truss braced below windows, ½″ vertical post tie rods, ½″ x 2″ inside truss bars, sheathed outside with ¾″ x 2″ poplar.

Roof. Monitor deck style extending over each vestibule with Empire ceiling of composite board (Agasote or artificial lumber at Purchaser's option) decorated in color and gold. Concealed steel rafter ⅜″ x 1½″ at each panel post. Covered with No. 8 canvas thoroughly painted and fitted with trolley platform over rear truck.

Vestibules. At each end with floors flush with car floor supported on main sills of car. Rear vestibule has 31″ single swing door, triple steps with brass binding, ¼″ steel plate hangers, Empire safety treads, and trap doors on each side; also 27″ swing door in end with spring buffers and train passage diaphragm. Front end has isolated platform for motorman, sliding door connecting with baggage room, 30″ swing door on left side, 3 sashes across front and switch cabinet in end bulkhead.

Interior Finish. Mahogany, with curved window heads and mouldings, inlaid marquetry borders in main panels, Empire ceiling, bronze trimmings, 9 rod bottom parcel racks.

Toilet Room. In left hand rear corner of car with dry hopper, cement floor and water cooler on outside.

Seats. 16 Heywood No. 327 AGF rattan covered seats with head-roll backs and bronze grab handles; also 3 corner seats with stationary backs.

Heater. Hot water, hot air or electric, supplied by Purchaser, or by Car Builder as specified by Purchaser at extra charge for same.

Windows. Lower side sashes fitted with Edwards' locks with concealed racks, Pantasote curtains with Forsyth fixtures. Deck sashes hung on Hart's ratchet fixtures.

Doors. 31″ swing door in rear body bulkhead; 22¾″ swing door in center partition; sliding door in front bulkhead; 20″ toilet room door swinging inward; 4′ 10″ sliding baggage door on each side.

Glass. ¼″ plate in all swing doors; tinted cathedral glass in Gothic and deck sasnes; selected D. S. A. car glass in lower window and bulkhead sashes.

Grab Handles. Of hickory in bronze sockets at each side of rear vestibule side doors, diagonal handle at same inclination as car steps on outside of doors, and iron handles at each side of baggage doors.

Lighting. Wire, switches, fuses, sockets and lamp brackets for 25 lamps (16 c. p.) are supplied and installed by Car Builder.

Draw Bars and Couplers. Automatic M. C. B. radial type on each end of car.

Track Sanders. Two compressed air type on front end of car.

Pilot. One locomotive style on front end, cut out for radial draw bar and supported on heavy steel angle braces.

Headlight. Supplied by Purchaser, wiring and brackets for same on front end of car by Car Builder.

Trolley Retriever. Supplied by Purchaser and attached by Car Builder.

Fare Register and Fittings. Installed by Car Builder if supplied by Purchaser.

Miscellaneous Fittings. Signal bell with cord and hangers, one 12″ alarm gong, emergency tools in case, switch iron, roof steps, mat and handles, illuminated sign in front end, brackets for tail and marker lamps, are supplied by Car Builder.

Painting. Color, lettering, numbers and striping as directed by Purchaser.

Hand Brakes. Lindstrom malleable iron ratchet lever on each end of car.

Air Brakes. Supplied by Purchaser and may be installed by Car Builder at extra charge for same.

Electric Power Equipment. Supplied and installed by Purchaser at destination, or may be installed by Car Builder at extra charge for same. Concealed portion of trolley cable only may be supplied and installed by Car Builder at extra cost of same.

Trucks. Baldwin Class 78-30-A with Standard 36″ M. C. B. section forged-rolled steel wheels on 5½″ hammered steel axles with 5″ x 9″ journals and prepared for G. E. No. 73—75 H. P. motors (or motors specified by Purchaser) are supplied by Car Builder. If cars can be delivered on track on their own wheels the bodies should be mounted on trucks at Car Works; otherwise by Purchaser at destination.

Prices can be quoted on duplicates of car as specified above, o with any exceptions desired. Detail specifications and drawings are submitted for Purchaser's approval before starting work.

45 FT. SINGLE END, THREE COMPARTMENT, COMBINATION PASSENGER, SMOKING AND BAGGAGE INTERURBAN CAR

Combined motorman's cab and baggage room at front end; smoking room seating 12 persons; main passenger compartment with toilet room in rear, and rear vestibule with steps and doors on each side.

This plan is very satisfactory for short interurban lines, frequent schedule, and quadruple 50 to 60 H. P. motors at maximum speed of 45 to 50 miles per hour.

A small baggage room with folding seats for smokers or over-flow crowds is desirable under most interurban conditions.

General Specifications and Dimensions

Length over buffers	45′ 0″	Distance between bolster centers	22′ 6″
Length over vestibules	43′ 8″	Wheel base of trucks	6′ 4″
Length of baggage room	10′ 0″	Seating capacity	40
Length of smoking room	8′ 2″	Length of seats	38¼″
Length of main compartment	20′ 5″	Width of aisle	20″
Length of rear vestibule	4′ 10″	Weight of car body, about	25,000 lbs.
Width over sheathing at sills	8′ 9½″	Weight of trucks, about	16,000 lbs.
Width over all (or to suit purchaser)	9′ 0″	Weight complete on track, including quadruple G. E. No. 80—40 H. P. Electrical equipment and air brakes, about	55,000 lbs.
Width inside	8′ 0½″		
Height, under sills to top of roof	9′ 5″		
Height, from track to top of roof	12′ 9″		

Bottom Frame. Double outside sills of 4½″x7¾″ and 1¾″x6″ yellow pine with ⅜″x7¾″ steel plate bolted between. Two center sills of 6″ steel I-beams. Two intermediate sills of yellow pine reinforced with steel plates under baggage room. Sills extend under vestibules from buffer to buffer. Two 10″ plate truss bolsters. Two 6″ I-needle beams. 6″x½″ end sill plates. ¾″ tie rod with turnbuckle in center at each cross sill.

Trusses. Two 1⅜″ under truss rods with 1¾″ turnbuckles and two ½″x2″ inside truss bars on pedestals over bolsters for supporting overhanging ends.

Floor. Double thickness of ⅞″x3¼″ yellow pine with waterproof building felt between.

Body. Pullman twin window style with alternate single and panel posts of oak, thoroughly bra_ed and sheathed with ¾″x2″ poplar; ½″ vertical tie rod at each post.

Roof. Monitor deck style with steam coach hoods; concealed steel rafter at each panel post; covered with No. 8 canvas, painted and fitted with trolley platform.

Combined Baggage Room and Motorman's Vestibule. At front end with 4-ft. baggage door on each side, 3 sashes across front and 22¼″ swing door in rear partition. Folding wooden seats hinged to walls wherever convenient.

Smoking Room. The length of 3 side windows with six cross seats and swing doors in partitions.

Rear Vestibule. With 31″ single swing door, triple steps and trap doors at each side. Three sashes across rear end.

Interior Finish. Cherry in natural grain, smooth "sanitary" finish with inlaid borders. Empire ceiling in color and gold. Polished bronze trimmings. Seven 46″ parcel racks. Oak with gloss finish in baggage room.

Toilet Room. In rear left-hand corner with Duner water flush closet, white enamel inside finish, cement floor, roof ventilator and water cooler in alcove on outside.

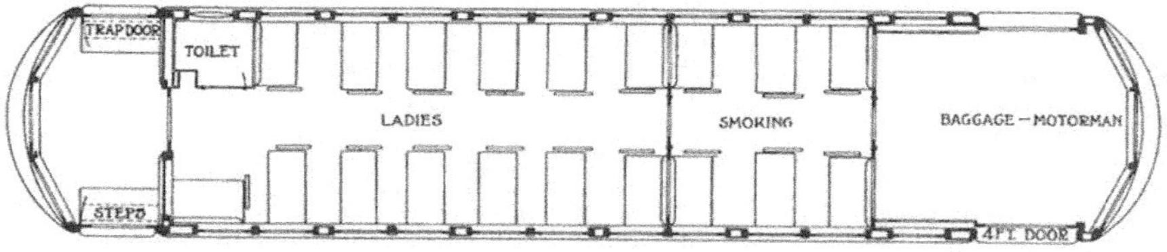

Drawing No. 447—Plan of 45 Ft. Three Compartment Interurban Car

Engraving No. 447—45 Ft. Single End Three Compartment Interurban Car

Seats. Eleven Hale & Kilburn's No. 10-A style with stationary 18″ backs with bronze grab handles, spring edge cushions, and upholstered with woven rattan, and eight corner seats with backs against partitions.

Windows. Single lower sashes fitted with Edwards' locks with concealed racks, lifts and springs. Stationary upper sashes of twin Gothic style. Deck sashes in 3 sections, the center ones hung on ratchet fixtures. Pantasote curtains on spring rollers with Forsyth fixtures.

Glass. Double strength selected car glass in all lower sashes and doors. Rippled cathedral glass in zinc channels in Gothic and deck sashes.

Window Guards. Body end windows protected by 3 rod bronze guards; lower side windows by 3 rod painted iron guards on outside.

Lighting. Wire, switches, fuses, sockets and lamp brackets for 25 lamps on separate bases and concealed portion of trolley cable, are supplied and installed by Car Builder.

Grab Handles. Hickory in malleable iron sockets at each side of rear steps; also horizontal bronze handle on each vestibule side door.

Drawbars and Couplers. On each end, automatic M. C. B. radial type.

Track Sanders. Two Nichols-Lintern compressed air style on front end.

Pilot. One locomotive style, under front end below radial drawbar.

Headlight. Supplied by Purchaser. Wiring and brackets for same on front end by Car Builder.

Trolley Retriever. One Knutson No. 2 on rear end of car.

Heater. Smith No. 2-C hot water style located in baggage room with pipes extending through passenger compartments.

Fare Register and Fittings. Supplied and installed by Purchaser, or by Car Builder at extra charge for same.

Miscellaneous Fittings. Signal bells with cord and hangers, alarm gongs, emergency tools, switch iron, roof steps, mats and handles, oil tail lamps and flags, are supplied by Car Builder.

Painting. Color, lettering, numbers and striping as directed by Purchaser.

Hand Brakes. In front end with malleable iron Lindstrom ratchet lever.

Air Brakes. Supplied by Purchaser and may be installed by Car Builder at extra charge for same.

Electric Power Equipment. Supplied and installed by Purchaser at destination, or may be installed by Car Builder at extra charge for same.

Trucks. Supplied and attached by Purchaser at destination, or by Car Builder at extra charge for same. If cars can be delivered on track on their own wheels, the trucks should be supplied and attached by Car Builder at Car Works.

Prices can be quoted on duplicates of car as specified above, or with any exceptions desired.

Detail specifications and drawings are submitted for Purchaser's approval before starting work.

62 FT. BUFFET OBSERVATION PARLOR CAR FOR EXTRA FARE LIMITED SERVICE

For use simply as a motor car or at rear end of trains. It corresponds to the Pullman equipment of steam roads; has continuous train passage and convertible motorman's cab at front end and large open observation platform with dome, awning and bronze rail at rear end.

For large systems competing with steam roads for first-class business, cars of this type are considered necessary.

BOTTOM FRAME. Two outside sills of $4\frac{1}{2}''$x$7\frac{1}{4}''$ and $17\frac{8}''$x$6''$ yellow pine with $\frac{5}{8}''$x$7\frac{1}{4}''$ steel plate bolted between. (Sill plates are of proper strength to support the weights attached to car body, viz.: A = same depth as side sills, $7\frac{3}{4}''$; B = from bottom of side sills to window sills, $30''$). C = from bottom of side sills to top of truss plank, $18''$. Four center and intermediate sills of $6''$ steel I-beams between yellow pine fillers extending from buffer to buffer, supported on and bolted to two $8''$ steel I-needle beams and two $10''$ steel plate bolsters with riveted steel channel fillers. $\frac{3}{4}''$ tie-rods with turnbuckles in center. $1\frac{1}{2}''$ under truss rods. $1\frac{1}{2}''$x$2''$ inside truss bars on pedestals over bolsters for supporting overhanging ends of car.

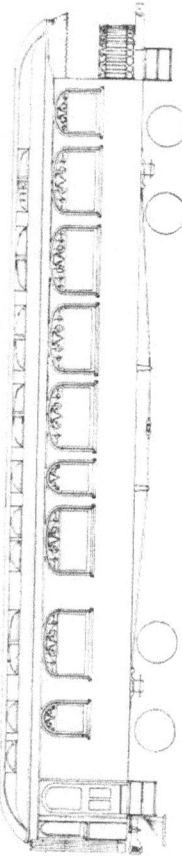

FLOOR. Double thickness with $\frac{1}{2}''$ Keystone Hair Insulator between, covered in parlor with removable green and gold Wilton carpet. Floor of all other compartments, including platforms and corridor, is covered with Greenwich inlaid linoleum cemented at edges.

BODY. Right-hand side is shown in engravings No. 443. Left side drawing 443, has six large windows with single sashes to raise; one low stationary sash window in observation platform and two small windows at ends of corridor. Side posts are of oak with $\frac{1}{2}''$ vertical tie-rods, fitted with truss bracing, filled with $\frac{7}{8}''$ poplar and $\frac{1}{2}''$ Keystone Hair Insulator, and sheathed outside with $\frac{1}{4}''$x$2''$ poplar continuous from sills to letter panels.

ROOF. Monitor deck style with steam coach hoods, concealed steel rafter at each side post, covered with No. 8 duck, thoroughly painted and fitted with trolley platform full length.

WINDOWS. All movable sashes are hung on Edwards' spring balance and fitted with Edwards' locks and rollers. Oval sashes are hinged at top with bronze fixtures at bottom. The upper sashes are stationary and double and between which the lower ones raise. All clear glass in car is heavy polished plate. Gothic and deck sashes are glazed with leaded art glass in metal frames. Holophane glass in all oval sashes. Deck sashes hung on ratchet fixtures.

Drawing No. 443—62 Ft. Observation Parlor Car—Left Side Elevation

Engraving No. 443—62 Ft. Buffet Observation Parlor Car—Right Side and Front View

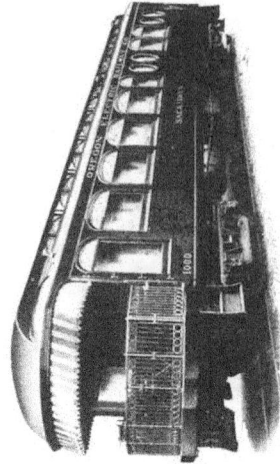

Rear End and Right Side View

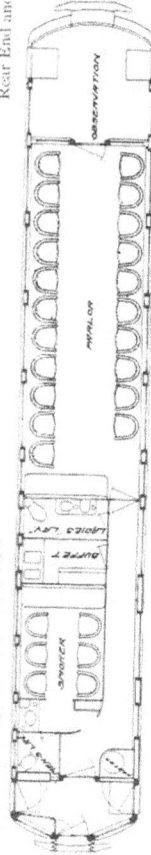

Drawing No. 443—Plan of 62 Ft. Observation Parlor Car

General Specifications and Dimensions

Length over buffers	62'	$1\frac{3}{4}''$
Length over vestibule and rail	59'	$10\frac{1}{2}''$
Length of car body	51'	$8''$
Length of front vestibule	4'	$0''$
Length of observation platform	8'	$4''$
Length of parlor	25'	$11''$
Length of smoking room	8'	$6''$
Length of buffet	3'	$3''$
Length of ladies' toilet	2'	$11''$
Width at sills, including sheathing	9'	$3\frac{3}{4}''$
Width over all	9'	$6''$
Width inside parlor	8'	$5''$
Width inside smoking room	6'	$9\frac{3}{4}''$
Width of corridor	2'	$3''$
Height, under sills to top of roof	9'	$6\frac{1}{2}''$
Height, track to top of roof	13'	$1''$
Distance between bolster centers	38'	$6''$
Wheel base of trucks	6'	$6''$
Seating capacity, (extra fares) not including observation platform	35	
Weight of car body, about	44,000 lbs.	
Weight of trucks	21,460 lbs.	
Weight complete on track, including quadruple G. E. No. 73—75 H. P. electric power equipment and air brakes, with full water tanks, about	44 tons	

Interior of Parlor from Observation Platform Looking Forward

DOORS. All doors are of the swing type. Front vestibule has 27″ single door on each side, also double folding door in center of end for train service. Each end of car body has 27″ door. Door in corridor swings in both directions. Doors are fitted with pneumatic checks wherever practical.

INTERIOR FINISH. Of selected dark figured mahogany in large smooth panels with inlaid border; of colored woods. Window heads are of same curvature over art glass sashes as on outside of car. Green silk Pantasote curtains are concealed in mahogany casings below Gothic windows and cover lower sashes only. Ceiling is of Empire style decorated in green and gold. Both toilet rooms and buffet are finished in white enamel. Vestibule and observation platform are finished in same manner as interior of car.

OBSERVATION PLATFORM. At rear end having large stationary window from truss plank to letter panel at each side, surrounded by polished solid bronze railing with gate at each side and in center as shown in engraving No. 443, dome in ceiling with 3 lamps concealed in opalescent shade, removable awning of 10-oz. duck hung from under side of hood, and supplied with six large folding camp chairs with carpet seats and backs.

PARLOR. Occupies full width of car at rear end next to observation platform, is fitted with four single sash windows and one coach side window on each side. Rear end bulkhead has stationary plate glass from truss plank to top of door in panel at each side of center door and in door. Front bulkhead has one large polished mahogany panel from corridor door to opposite side of car with green plush sofa and head-roll back covering lower part of bulkhead. Parlor is furnished with ten No. 16-P and eleven No. 19-P Heywood Bros. & Wakefield Co.'s white reed chairs with dark green plush cushions, head-rolls, arms and chafing bindings; also one sofa against front bulkhead similarly upholstered.

SMOKING ROOM. Located as shown in drawing No. 443, with heavy mahogany colored portieres hung on brass rods and rings across openings between men's lavatory and corridor, and furnished with six No. 16-P mahogany colored reed chairs upholstered with dark green leather, also one sofa against bulkhead full width of compartment and finished in similar manner.

BUFFET. Next to smoking room, with 22″ door to corridor, oval window at opposite side and deck sash in roof, furnished with sink, having hot, and cold water spigots and ice-chest underneath, linen closet, drawer, locker, plate and glass racks, shelf, nickel plated hot water urn and a two-burner alcohol stove.

LADIES' TOILET AND LAVATORY. Next to parlor, with door to corridor, oval window, deck sash and Globe ventilator in roof. Fitted with air pressure water flush hopper, nickeline wash-stand with hot and cold water spigots, soap dish, towel racks, comb and brush rack, coat hooks, nickeline water cooler and bevel edge mirror.

MEN'S TOILET. In right-hand front corner of car furnished same as ladies' room except with separate lavatory.

MEN'S LAVATORY. Between men's toilet and smoking room, fitted with nickeline wash-stand, racks, hooks, cooler, etc., same as ladies' lavatory, except mirror in toilet room door full size of center panel.

HEATER AND CABINET. In left-hand front corner of car, with curved front and door opening in corridor, lined with asbestos and galvanized iron, fitted with Peter Smith No. 2-C hot water heater with pipes along truss plank, also with 20 gallon air pressure hot water tank suspended above heater.

MOTORMAN'S CAB. At right side of front vestibule formed by swinging door which isolates the motorman when longitudinal of car and encloses controlling apparatus when transverse of car. Outside door at right-hand side has drop sash in upper part. Bulkhead in rear of motorman's cab contains an asbestos-lined cabinet for switches, fuses and other electric equipment.

TRAIN PASSAGE AND BUFFERS. At front end of car supported at top and bottom on four spring plungers is fitted a steel chafing frame connected with end door by plaited diaphragm so as to form closed passage when coupled to cars similarly equipped. Buffers are beveled at ends so as to automatically compress when on tangent. The end doors are locked when on city curves. Rear platform has similar spring buffer at bottom only with sliding apron on platform.

DRAWBARS AND COUPLERS. Automatic M. C. B. radial type on each end of car for 50 feet radius curves.

PILOT. Locomotive style with front buffer heel braced with 2½″ steel angles.

LIGHTING. Wire, switches, fuses, sockets and lamp fixtures for lighting and concealed portion of trolley cable, are supplied and installed by Car Builder. Parlor has three 5-lamp fixtures at destination. Parlor has three 5-lamp fixtures and 12 wall brackets with bronze husks as shown in interior view. Smoker has one 5-lamp fixture and 2 wall brackets. Front vestibule has one 2-lamp fixture concealed in opalescent hemisphere. Corridor roof has 3 single lamp brackets. Observation platform has three-lamp fixture in dome and two wall brackets. Toilet rooms, lavatory and buffet each have one lamp.

WINDOW GUARDS. Polished bronze on interior of car only. Glass around observation platform protected by large single bronze rails. Swing doors and corridor windows have bronze guards. Windows in rear of parlor have bronze foot rails.

GRAB HANDLES. Each vestibule and corner post is fitted with a solid bronze vertical grab handle, also similar one diagonally on outside of each front vestibule side door.

HEADLIGHT. Supplied by Purchaser. Bracket support on hood over front vestibule and wiring by Car Builder.

STEPS. Each corner of car fitted with triple steps with ¾″ steel hangers; wooden treads covered with safety treads; edges fitted with brass binding and step openings covered with Edwards' self-raising steel trap doors.

TABLES. Eight mahogany tables with folding leg, at one end and bronze hooks at other end, are carried in table locker in men's lavatory. Bronze table wall sockets are conveniently located in walls of parlor and smoking room.

WATER SUPPLY AND PLUMBING. Two 100-gallon steel air pressure water storage tanks are hung under car, encased to prevent freezing, and connected by heavy galvanized pipe with closets, wash-stands, sink, water coolers, hot water tank and air pressure tank. The air pressure tank and air reducing valve are supplied by Purchaser with air brake equipment.

PARCEL RACKS. Sectional, rod bottom style of polished solid bronze, conveniently located in parlor and smoking room.

TRIMMINGS. Polished solid bronze both inside and outside of car (oxidized finish at Purchaser's option).

MISCELLANEOUS FITTINGS. Bronze motorman's roof steps, roof mat and handles, one 12″ alarm gong, air signal with cord, etc. Emergency tools in glass front case, tool and supply box hung under car floor. Six corner brackets for signal lamps and flags are supplied and attached by Car Builder.

PAINTING. Color, lettering, numbers and striping as directed by Purchaser.

HAND BRAKES. Polished solid bronze Lindstrom lever, shaft tube, ratchet wheel and dog, in left-hand side of front vestibule and attached to bronze rail on rear platform.

AIR BRAKES. Supplied by Purchaser and installed by Car Builder. Westinghouse A. M. R. single end control with D3-E. G. compressor, reducing valve and pressure tank for water, whistle and air signal.

ELECTRIC POWER EQUIPMENT. Supplied and installed by Purchaser at destination, or may be installed by Car Builder at extra charge for same.

TRUCKS. Baldwin Class 78-30-B with Standard 36″ M. C. B. section rolled steel wheels on 5½″ hammered steel axles with 5″x9″ journals and prepared for G. E. No. 73 motors, are supplied and attached to car body by Car Builder and delivered on track ready for transportation on own wheels in steam railroad trains to destination. If cars cannot be delivered on their own wheels, the trucks should be attached to car bodies by Purchaser at destination.

Price can be quoted on duplicates of car as specified above, or with any exceptions desired.

Detail specifications and drawings are submitted for Purchaser's approval before starting work.

BOTTOM FRAME. Two outside sills of 5″x8″, yellow pine with ⅞″x8″ steel plate bolted to outside full length of car. Four center and intermediate sills of 8″, steel I-beams between yellow pine fillers. All supported on and bolted to two 8″ steel I-needle beams and two 10″ steel plate truss bolsters. Under truss rods 1¼″ diameter with 1¼″ turnbuckles. Nine ¾″ tie rods with turnbuckles in center.

FLOOR. 2″ oak planks laid crosswise and painted on both sides.

CONTROLLING CAB. Located in center of car platform occupying space 6′ 0″ long and 4′ 0″ wide on car floor with clear space on each side 2′ 0″ high for carrying poles, rails and other long articles. Floor of cab is 28″ above car floor. The space between car platform and cab floor is occupied by air compressor and other electrical equipment, which are better protected from dust and water than when hung under the car.

The cab proper is 8′ 0″ wide over sheathing, about same width as car platform over all, 6′ 0″ long, 7′ 4″ high, and 9′ 4″ from car platform to top of roof. Total height from track to top of cab 13′ 6″.

Each side of cab fitted with 20″ swing door and sliding sash window. Two single sash windows in each end of cab.

Roof covered with canvas and thoroughly painted.

LIGHTING. Cab is wired with sockets for one circuit of five lamps and headlight with bracket at each end. Headlight and lamps supplied by Purchaser at destination.

GRAB HANDLES. Painted iron, vertical at each side of each door, horizontal under each window on outside.

DRAWBARS AND COUPLERS. Automatic M. C. B. radial style at each end of car.

TRACK SANDERS. Two Nichols-Lintern air sanders with valve in each end of cab.

FENDER OR PILOT. Is composed of a switchman's platform or running board extending around each end of car, supported on heavy wrought iron brackets, and with iron hand rail around each end buffer.

TROLLEY RETRIEVER. If used, is supplied by Purchaser.

HEATER. If used in cab, is supplied and installed by Purchaser.

MISCELLANEOUS FITTINGS. Two 12″ alarm gongs, one switch iron, four tail light lens or corner brackets for oil lamps and flags, are supplied by Car Builder.

STAKES AND POCKETS. Ten on each side of car, securely bolted to side sills.

PAINTING. Color, lettering and numbers as directed by Purchaser.

HAND BRAKES. One horizontal iron wheel located in center of cab with chain, lever, etc. Supplied by Purchaser and may be installed by Car Builder at extra charge for same, or by Purchaser at destination.

ELECTRIC POWER EQUIPMENT. Supplied and installed by Purchaser at destination, or may be installed by Car Builder at extra charge for same.

TRUCKS. Supplied and attached by Purchaser at destination, or by Car Builder at extra charge for same. If cars can be delivered on track on their own wheels, the trucks should be supplied and attached by Car Builder at Car Works.

Prices can be quoted on duplicates of cars as specified above, or with any exceptions desired.

Detail specifications and drawings are submitted for Purchaser's approval before starting work.

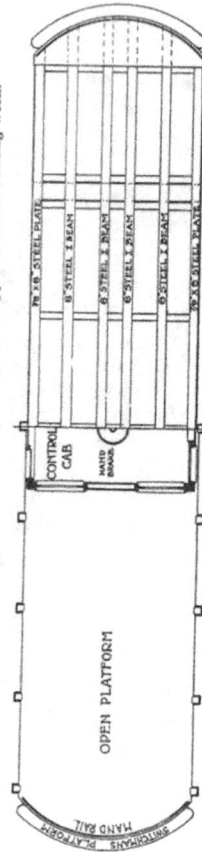

Drawing No. 449—Plan of 40 Ft. Construction Car and Locomotive

Engraving No. 449—40 Ft. Construction Car and Electric Locomotive

40 FT. CONSTRUCTION, FREIGHT, LINE AND GENERAL UTILITY CAR AND ELECTRIC LOCOMOTIVE

The large controlling cab is in center, thus insuring the placing of all heavy loads directly over the trucks. It is elevated above the car floor, allowing ample space at each side for carrying poles, rails and other long material. It affords the motorman a clear view in all directions over bulky freight, and provides a space under the cab floor for air compressor and other equipment and tools. A platform can be placed on roof of cab for line construction and repair.

Instead of pilots or fenders, switchman's running boards with hand rails extend around each end for convenience in coupling and switching work. One or more cars of this type can be used economically on most electric railways:

General Specifications and Dimensions

Length over buffers	40′ 0″	
Width over sills	8′ 4″	
Width over all (or to suit Purchaser)	8′ 10″	
Distance between bolster centers	23′ 0″	
Wheel base of trucks	6′ 4″	
Weight of car body, about	16,000 lbs.	
Weight of trucks, about	16,000 lbs.	
Weight complete on track, including quadruple G. E. No. 80—40 H. P. electrical equipment and air brakes	46,000 lbs.	

13

44 FT. DOUBLE END, SUBURBAN AND LIGHT INTERURBAN CAR WITH SMOKING COMPARTMENT

Double sliding doors in each end and double folding doors on each side of each vestibule facilitate quick loading and discharging passengers. The seating capacity is 48 persons with standing capacity about the same.

This is a very satisfactory car for suburban and short interurban traffic, but where it is desirable that it resemble street cars in general appearance. 40 to 50 H.P. motors and maximum speed of 35 to 40 miles per hour. If used for platform prepayment, curved rails extend from center of end doors to center of steps to separate entrance from exit.

General Specifications and Dimensions

Length over buffers	44′ 00″	Height, under sills to top of roof	9′ 0″
Length over vestibules	42′ 7¾″	Height, from track to top of roof	12′ 2¼″
Length of car body	32′ 7¾″	Distance between bolster centers	21′ 4″
Length of vestibules	5′ 0″	Wheel base of trucks	6′ 0″
Length of main compartment	21′ 4″	Seating capacity	48
Length of smoking compartment	10′ 8″	Length of seats	35½″
Width over panels at sills	8′ 3″	Width of aisle	19″
Width over side posts	8′ 5″	Weight of car body, about	17,500 lbs.
Width over all	8′ 7″	Weight of trucks (2)	15,860 lbs.
		Total weight on track ready for service	24 tons

Bottom Frame. Two outside sills of 4½″ x 7¾″ and 1¾″ x 6″ yellow pine with ⅝″ x 7¾″ (⅜″ x 12″ at purchaser's option) steel plate bolted between. Two center sills of 6″ steel I-beams filled with yellow pine. End sills re-enforced with ½″ x 6″ steel plates, platform sills with ½″ x 5″ steel plates, buffers covered with ⅜″ x 8″ steel plates, 10″ steel plate truss bolsters. One 6″ I-needle beam in center. Eleven ⅝″ tie rods full width of bottom.

Trusses. Two 1¼″ under truss rods with 1½″ turnbuckles and two ⅜″ x 2½″ inside truss bars on pedestals over bolsters for supporting overhanging ends.

Floor. Double thickness of ⅞″ x 3¼″ yellow pine with water-proof building felt between and covered in aisle with longitudinal floor strips.

Body. Single side post style with 12 side windows and curved panels beneath. Outside sheathing of poplar. The car is made to resemble street cars so as not to be objectionable on city streets, but is framed heavier and stronger for interurban service.

Roof. Monitor deck style with detachable hoods, eleven ½″ x 1¼″ steel carlines, covered with No. 8 canvas thoroughly painted and fitted with trolley platform full length of deck. (This car can be made with single arch roof having ventilators in top.)

Vestibules. At each end, with floors 8 inches below car floor. Double folding doors, double steps with safety treads and trap door over step opening, at each side of each vestibule. Three drop sashes in each end. If a prepayment system of fare collection be used reversible curved railings extend from center of body end doors to centers of step openings.

Doors. Each end of car body has 38″ double sliding doors operating independently of each other. Smoking partition has 24″ door to swing in both directions.

Interior Finish. Of mahogany in smooth "sanitary" design. Monitor deck ceiling of 3-ply veneer painted and decorated. Solid bronze interior trimmings.

Heaters. Six electric heaters; four in ladies' compartment and two in smoking room, are supplied and installed complete by Car Builder.

Seats. Ladies' compartment furnished with twelve Hale & Kilburn No. 199-A reversible back spring rattan steel seats with bronze grab handle and four stationary back corner seats. Smoking compartment has longitudinal rattan seats with 4′ 8″ aisle between. See plan No. 468.

Windows. Twelve side windows with stationary upper sashes, lower sashes to raise and fitted with bronze locks, lifts, springs, etc. Twelve deck sashes on each side hung on Harts' ratchets and fitted with spring catches. Pantasote curtains with Forsyth No. 88 fixtures.

Glass. Wire glass in deck sashes. Chipped glass in smoking partition. All other windows and doors have selected double-strength American car glass.

Window Guards. Of 3-rod ½″ bronze tube protect inside bulkhead windows.

Grab Handles. Both sides of all steps are fitted with 30″ hickory handles in malleable iron sockets.

Lighting. Wire, switches, fuses and sockets for 20 lamps on separate bases, also concealed portion of trolley cable, are supplied and installed by Car Builder.

Draw Bars and Couplers. Rigid steel coupling pocket bolted to each buffer with 6′ coupling bar carried on hooks under side of car. Automatic radial couplers may be supplied at extra charge for same.

Track Sanders. One compressed air sander on each end of car.

Fender or Pilot. Supplied by Purchaser and installed by Car Builder, or may be supplied by Car Builder at extra charge for same.

Headlight. One G. E. luminous arc style with wiring and bracket at each end, supplied and installed by Car Builder.

Trolley Retrievers. One Knutson No. 2 on each end of car supplied and attached by Car Builder.

Fare Register and Fittings. Supplied and installed by Purchaser, or by Car Builder at extra charge for same.

Miscellaneous Fittings. Two 12″ alarm gongs, two signal bells with cord and hangers, emergency tools, two Armspear signal lamps and flags with corner brackets, switch iron and two holders, electric signal bells with push buttons and batteries, twelve leather hand straps in smoking compartment, roof steps, mat and handle at each end of car, are supplied and attached by Car Builder.

Painting. Color, lettering, numbers and striping as directed by Purchaser.

Hand Brakes. Peacock C. Drum with bronze ratchet windlass in each vestibule.

Air Brakes. Double-end straight air equipment supplied by Purchaser and may be installed by Car Builder at cost plus 10 per cent.

Electric Power Equipment. Quadruple 40 H.P. motors with double end K control, supplied by Purchaser and may be installed by Car Builder at cost of same plus 10 per cent.

Trucks. Baldwin Class 72-18-A with 33″, 500-lb. cast-iron wheels with 3½″ tread, on 5″ hammered steel axles with 4¼″ x 8″ journals, and prepared for G.E. No. 88 motors, are supplied by Car Builder. If cars can be delivered on track on their own wheels, the bodies should be mounted on trucks at car works, otherwise by Purchaser at destination.

Prices can be quoted on duplicates of car as specified above, or with any exceptions desired. Detail specifications and drawings are submitted for Purchaser's approval before starting work.

Engraving No. 468—44 Ft. "Double End" Suburban and Light Interurban, Two Compartment Car

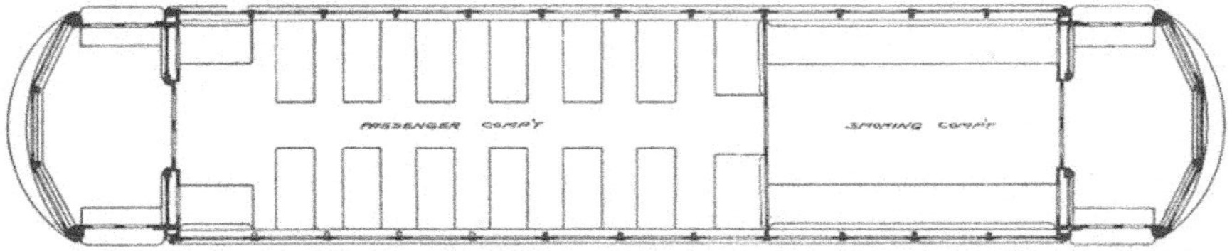

Drawing No. 468—Plan of 44 Ft. Two Compartment, "Double End" Suburban Car.

Engraving No. 468—Interior of 44 Ft. Two Compartment Suburban Car.

Engraving No. 465—Interior View Through Smoking Compartment, Center Vestibule and Ladies' Compartment of the "Oklahoma" Car.

End View

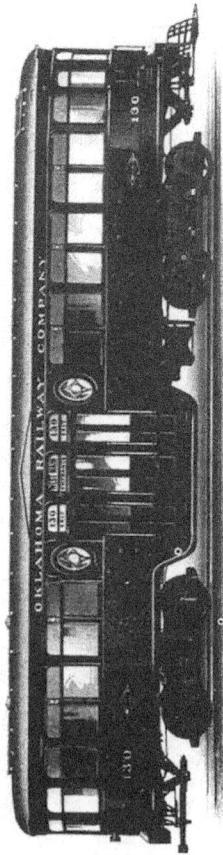

Engraving No. 465—18 Ft. Center Vestibule, Arch Roof, Steel, Prepayment Car.

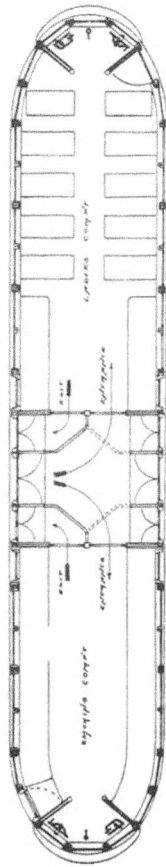

Drawing No. 465—Plan of 48 Ft. Center Vestibule, Prepayment, Two Compartment, Double End Car.

THE "OKLAHOMA" CAR

48 FT. CENTER VESTIBULE, DOUBLE END, STEEL CAR WITH WOOD LININGS, WITH SMOKING COMPARTMENT; FOR CITY, SUBURBAN AND LIGHT INTERURBAN SERVICE

These cars were designed by and built under the supervision of officers of The Oklahoma Railway Company, and include the latest ideas in design, details and construction of electric cars.

Their principal advantages are as follows:

INCREASED CAPACITY WITH LESS WEIGHT. One center vestibule, always used for the same purpose, is substituted for the usual two large end platforms alternately used for fare collection or car control and not exclusively designed for either. The seats extend to each end of car providing greater seating capacity (54). The step openings at devil strip side are closed with trap doors affording standing space *back of the conductor* after prepayment of fares. Elimination of long overhanging end platforms reduces weight and imposes the greatest load in center of car where it is more easily supported.

ABSOLUTE COLLECTION OF ALL FARES. As there are no end platforms and no steps outside of the car all passengers must *enter* the car. Even in rush hours when *the inside steps are crowded* they are within reaching distance and directly under the eye of the conductor so *all* passengers must either have passed and paid the conductor or are within his reach while at his station.

INCREASED MILEAGE OF CARS. Owing to quicker and unobstructed movement of passengers in each direction simultaneously. All enter at the 3-ft. center door, pay fare and turn to right or left to ladies' or smoking compartment, at the same time two unobstructed lines of passengers are leaving by the 27-inch separate exit doors from each compartment. The average distance and time consumed from seats to exits is reduced and time saved.

REDUCED ACCIDENTS AND DAMAGES. The only entrance and exits for passengers are always directly in front of the conductor when at his permanent station, and errors in starting cars are without excuse. The side doors may be operated by hand by the conductor and left open on the curb side in mild weather; under manual control by levers, or pneumatic control by valves at the conductor's stand. The motorman is relieved from exit door control and devotes his whole attention to safe operation of his car. He has a separate door for his exclusive use at each end of car.

SMOKING AND SEPARATION OF PASSENGERS. On long runs a smoking room entirely separate from ladies' compartment is desirable. Ladies and workmen in soiled clothing usually prefer to be separated. In Southern cities this plan can be used for separation of races.

PROTECTION OF EMPLOYEES FROM WEATHER. Both motorman and conductor are housed at all times and protected from weather. The motorman is separated from passengers by railings or bulkheads and curtains for excluding light. This space at rear end is utilized by standing passengers.

Standard interurban cars of same passenger capacity weigh about 5 ton more than this car. It costs about $100. per ton per annum for power, therefore, the saving in current soon offsets the increased first cost of this construction.

General Specifications and Dimensions

Length over buffers	48' 7⅜"
Length of body	47' 7⅜"
Length of center vestibule	7' 6"
Length of ladies' compartment	21' 6"
Length of smoking compartment	17' 8"
Width at sills including panels	8' 5"
Width over all (can be made to suit Purchaser)	8' 9"
Height under center sills to top of roof	8' 10¼"
Height inside from floor to ceiling	7' 8½"
Height from track to top of roof	11' 6½"
Distance between bolster centers	26' 0¾"
Wheel base of trucks	6' 4"
Seating capacity	54
Length of cross seats	36"
Width of aisle	20"
Weight of car body	22,000 lbs.
Weight of trucks	16,132 lbs.
Weight on track, complete, including Westinghouse quadruple No. 101-B 40 H.P. motor equipment and air brakes, about	26 tons

Ready for Sand Blasting Steel Sheathing and/or Painting.

Steel Frame Ready for Steel Belt Rail and Sheathing.

Steel Bottom Frame.

BOTTOM FRAME. All steel underframe composed of 2 center sills of 8" steel I-beams, 2 outside sills of 6" channels bent downward at centers under step openings, bent continuous around ends of car and re-enforced and spliced near bolsters. Bolsters are of the double channel or box type of built-up I-beams between center and side sills with 12" cover plates and re-enforced in centers. Cross framing is of built-up I-beams. 8" at center sills and 6" at side sills. Diagonal sills are 4" I-beams. All parts are riveted together with corner angles and gusset plates. See engraving above.

BODY FRAME. Twin window style with curved upper corners. Posts of 3" I-beams riveted to side sills, belt rails, top plate and side sheathing. Top plate of $3\frac{1}{2}$" x 2" x $\frac{1}{4}$" angle continuous around ends and sides of car and re-enforced at splices. Belt rail of 2" x $1\frac{1}{2}$" x $\frac{1}{4}$" angles around ends and sides of car except, at door openings. Outside sheathing of $\frac{1}{8}$" sheet steel on sides and $\frac{7}{8}$" around ends, with joints covered by $\frac{1}{32}$" x 3" steel battens riveted through sheathing and body frame. Outside steel panels are thoroughly sand blasted before painting.

FLOOR. Wood nailing sills are bolted to steel frame. Double floor of $\frac{7}{8}$" yellow pine with water-proof building felt between, thoroughly painted on both sides. Hard wood longitudinal strips in aisles.

ROOF. Single arch style. Sixteen $\frac{1}{2}$" x $1\frac{1}{2}$" steel rafters bent to shape of roof and bolted to side plates and wooden carlines which are covered with $\frac{1}{16}$" poplar and No. 6 canvas thoroughly painted, fitted with trolley platform full length, ceiled inside with veneer, painted and decorated. See interior view.

VENTILATION. Free circulation of air between roof and ceiling is obtained from 4 ventilators at each end set in panels over end windows. See end view. Roof is fitted with a Globe ventilator with bronze registers in ceiling for every 4 lineal feet of car body. All end and lower side sashes can be lowered and secured at any height leaving any desired opening at top for additional ventilation.

VESTIBULE. Located near center of car with 36" entrance in center, 27" exit on each side, double swing doors, and Edwards' self-raising steel trap doors at each opening on both sides of car. Two reversible railings pivoted to door posts in end bulkheads form separate passages for entrance and exit on curb side of car and leave free passage between all compartments on devil strip side. The conductor's station is in center of vestibule facing curb side steps with fare box, register, or door control before him. The floor between steps is flush with the car floor. All steps are covered with safety treads. See plan No. 465.

DOORS. All side doors swing inward. They may be opened on curb side, closed on devil strip side and operated as an open platform if so desired. The compartments being protected by the bulkhead doors. The doors may be swung by manual or pneumatic control from the conductor's stand (at extra charge for same) and transverse bulkheads omitted if used under any of the prepayment systems. Any and all licenses and royalties for fare collection and door control, are paid by the Purchaser and the Car Builder held harmless. Independent double sliding doors operated by passengers are between vestibule and both compartments.

INTERIOR FINISH. Selected mahogany in smooth polished panels. Below windows of tongue and groove mahogany sheathing. Single arch ceiling in neat panels. Polished bronze interior trimmings. Bulkhead windows are protected by bronze guards.

HEATERS. Ten electric heaters complete, are supplied and installed by Car Builder.

SEATS. Ladies' compartment has 10 mahogany seats with reversible backs and bronze grab handles, two 6' 4" corner seats and two folding corner seats against motorman's cab. Smoking compartment has longitudinal seats and backs of mahogany with folding portion against motorman's door.

WINDOWS. Ten twin style, 3 single and 2 oval windows on each side and, 3 single style across each end. Upper sashes stationary, lower ones drop and are fitted with locks to hold them at any height. Pantasote curtains with Forsyth No. 88 fixtures at side windows and motorman's bulkheads. End center windows have single sashes.

GLASS. Oval windows glazed with leaded bevel plate glass. All other sashes and doors glazed with D.S.A. glass. Upper twin windows have leaded art glass in center to hide post.

GRAB HANDLES. Each side of all steps has hickory grab handle in bronze sockets. Motorman's doors have malleable iron handle on each side and iron stirrup beneath.

LIGHTING. Wire, switches, fuses, sockets, conduits and conduits for 25 lamps on separate bases, also concealed portion of trolley cable, are supplied and installed by Car Builder.

DRAW BARS AND COUPLERS. Supplied by purchaser, or may be supplied and installed by Car Builder at extra charge for same.

BUFFERS. On each end, a special wide buffer with bevel top for protection from both city and interurban cars.

TRACK SANDERS. Two compressed air style on each end of car.

FENDER OR PILOT. Supplied by Purchaser, or may be supplied and attached by Car Builder at extra charge for same.

HEADLIGHT. Supplied by Purchaser. Car Builder places wiring and brackets for same on each end of car.

TROLLEY RETRIEVER. Knutson No. 2 type on each end of car.

FARE REGISTER AND FITTINGS, OR FARE BOX. Supplied by Purchaser.

HUNTER SIGNS. If required, are supplied and fitted by Car Builder at extra charge for same.

MISCELLANEOUS FITTINGS. Two 12" alarm gongs, two 5" signal bells, electric bells, push buttons and batteries, hand poles and leather straps in smoking compartment, advertising moulding, combination motorman's seat and tool box, switch iron, dash sign holders, roof steps, mat and handle are supplied by Car Builder.

PAINTING. Color, lettering, numbers and striping as directed by Purchaser.

HAND BRAKES. Vertical geared iron wheel with shaft, supports and chain at each end of car.

AIR BRAKES. Supplied by Purchaser and may be installed by Car Builder at extra charge for same.

ELECTRIC POWER EQUIPMENT. Supplied and installed by Purchaser at destination, or may be installed by Car Builder at extra charge for same.

TRUCKS. Supplied and attached by Purchaser at destination, or by Car Builder at extra charge for same. If cars can be delivered on track on their own wheels the bodies should be mounted on trucks at car works; otherwise by Purchaser at destination.

Prices can be quoted on duplicates of car as specified above, or with any exceptions desired. Detail specifications and drawings are submitted for Purchaser's approval before starting work.

51. FT. SINGLE END PASSENGER AND SMOKING INTERURBAN CAR

Designed for running with same end forward at all times. Passengers' steps and doors at right side of front vestibule and both sides of rear end. Smoking room at front end. Main passenger compartment containing toilet and heater cabinet at rear end.

This car is suitable for four 75 H.P. motors, speed of 60 miles per hour, and is one of the most satisfactory types for long interurban railways.

General Specifications and Dimensions

Length of buffers	54'	4"
Length over vestibules	50'	0"
Length of car body	40'	2"
Length of front vestibule	11'	10"
Length of rear vestibule	5'	0"
Length of smoking room	12'	0"
Length of main compartment	28'	2"
With car at sills, including panels	8'	5½"
Width over all (can be made to suit	8'	8"
Height, under sills to top of roof.	9'	5"
Height, track to top of roof.	12'	11½"
Distance between bolster centers	28'	2"
Wheel base of trucks.	6'	6"
Seating capacity		52
Length of seats		36"
Width of aisle		26"
Weight of car body		20½"
Weight of trucks		26,500 lbs.
Total weight on track ready for service		18,600 lbs.
including quadruple Westinghouse No. 304, 90 H.P. motor equipment and air brakes		32 ton

BOTTOM FRAME. Two outside sills of 4½" x 7¾" and 13¼" x 6" yellow pine with ⅜" x 7¾" steel plate bolted between 8" steel channel at Purchaser's option. Two center sills of 6" steel I-beams. Two intermediate sills of yellow pine re-enforced at ends with ½" x 6" steel plates. ¾" tie rod with turnbuckle at center at each cross sill, full width of car. Two 10" steel plate truss bolsters. Two 6" I-needle beams. End sill plates ⅜" x 6" (this car can be made with all-steel bottom frame steel posts and steel plate truss sheathing below windows.)

TRUSSES. Two 1½" under truss rods with 1¾" turnbuckles and two ½" x 2" inside truss bars on pedestals over bolsters for supporting overhanging ends.

FLOOR. Double thickness ⅞" x 3¼" yellow pine with water-proof building felt between.

BODY. Pullman twin window style with alternate single and panel post of oak, thoroughly trussed below windows. ½" vertical tie rod at each post and sheathed outside with ¾ x 2" poplar.

ROOF. Monitor deck style with steam coach hoods, concealed steel rafter at each panel post, covered with No. 8 canvas, thoroughly painted and fitted with trolley platform over rear truck. (This car can be made with single arch roof having ventilators on top.)

VESTIBULES. With doors about 6" below car floor, supported on four 6" steel I-beams, with 8" channel buffers. Each side of rear end and right side of front end are fitted with 31" swing door, double steps with ¾" steel plate bolted between 8" steel channel at Purchaser's option. Sash in center of front vestibule is stationary, all other vestibule end sashes raise.

DOORS. Rear end of body has 30" single sliding door 3" off center toward right side. Front end has 28" door 9" off center toward step. Smoking partition has 28" sliding door in center which allows bulkhead seats to be same length as others and aisle same width full length of car.

INTERIOR FINISH. Polished mahogany in large smooth panels with borders of inlaid lines; semi-empire ceiling in color with gold striping; solid bronze trimmings; thirteen 38" rod bottom parcel racks.

TOILET ROOM. In rear left hand corner, with dry hopper cement floor, white enamel interior and roof ventilator.

HEATER AND CABINET. Smith No. 2-C hot water heater in asbestos and zinc lined cabinet against toilet room, with 1½" water pipes.

SEATS. Ladies' compartment has 14 Hale & Kilburn's No. 10-C plush seats with stationary head roll backs with grab handles, and 4 corner seats. Smoking room has similar seats in dark green leather. See drawing plan No. 466.

WINDOWS. Single lower side sashes fitted with Edwards' locks with concealed racks, lifts and springs. Thirteen deck sashes have hinges and separate bronze openers; others are stationary. Pantasote curtains on spring rollers with Forsyth fixtures.

GLASS. All body lower sashes glazed with D.S.A. glass. Gothic sashes with etched decorations in center. Chipped glass in deck sashes, toilet and heater cabinet windows. Plate glass in all doors and vestibule end sashes.

WINDOW GUARDS. Body end windows protected by 3 rod bronze guards; lower side windows by 4 rod painted iron guards on outside.

GRAB HANDLES. Hickory in malleable iron sockets, or one piece malleable iron at each side of all steps; also horizontal one piece handle on outside of all vestibule doors.

LIGHTING. Wire, switches, fuses, sockets and lamp brackets for 35 lamps on separate bases and concealed portion of trolley cable, are supplied and installed by Car Builder.

DRAW BARS AND COUPLERS. Niles radial draw bar with Hovey style coupler on each end of car, or heavy steel rigid coupling pocket on each buffer with 6-ft. coupling bar carried on hooks under side of car. Automatic couplers may be supplied at extra charge by Car Builder.

TRACK SANDERS. Two compressed air sanders on front end of car.

FENDER OR PILOT. Supplied by Purchaser and installed by Car Builder.

HEADLIGHT. Supplied by Purchaser.

TROLLEY RETRIEVER. Supplied by Purchaser. Wiring and bracket for same on front end of car, by Car Builder.

FARE REGISTER AND FITTINGS. Supplied by Purchaser, and installed by Car Builder.

MISCELLANEOUS FITTINGS. Signal bells with cord and hangers, one 12" alarm gong, emergency tools, switch iron, roof steps, mat and handles, two red lens on rear end, and illuminated sign on front end, are supplied by Purchaser.

PAINTING. Color, lettering, numbers and striping as directed by Purchaser.

HAND BRAKES. Peacock "C" drum with bronze ratchet windlass on front end of car.

AIR BRAKES. Supplied by Purchaser and may be installed by Purchaser at destination, or may be installed by Car Builder at extra charge for same.

ELECTRIC POWER EQUIPMENT. Supplied and installed by Purchaser at destination, or may be installed by Car Builder at extra charge for same.

TRUCKS. Baldwin Class 78-25-A with Standard 37" forged-rolled steel wheels with rims 3" thick and treads 3" wide on 5½" hammered-steel axles with 4½" x 8" journals and prepared for Westinghouse No. 304 motors, are supplied by Car Builder. If cars can be delivered on track on their own wheels the bodies should be mounted on wheels at car works; otherwise by Purchaser at destination. Detail specifications and drawings are submitted for Purchaser's approval before starting work. Prices can be quoted on duplicates of car as specified above, or with any exceptions desired.

Engraving No. 466—51 Ft. Single End, Two Compartment, Fast Interurban Car.

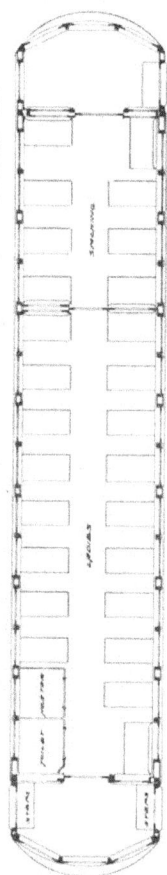

Drawing No. 466—Plan of Single End, Two Compartment Interurban Car with Toilet and Heater Cabinet.

Engraving No. 466—Interior of Two Compartment Interurban Car with Semi-Empire Ceiling.

51 FT. "SINGLE END" INTERURBAN COMBINATION PASSENGER AND BAGGAGE CAR

For running with same end forward at all times, with steps for passengers at each side of rear vestibule only, door for baggage and employes at each side of front end, with main passenger room in rear, smoking room and combined baggage-vestibule at front end, having iron railing for separating motorman from baggage. This plan has proven very satisfactory on many interurban lines on which all cars carry baggage for the convenience of passengers and handle first-class package express matter. It is suitable for four 75 H. P. motors and a maximum speed of 60 miles per hour.

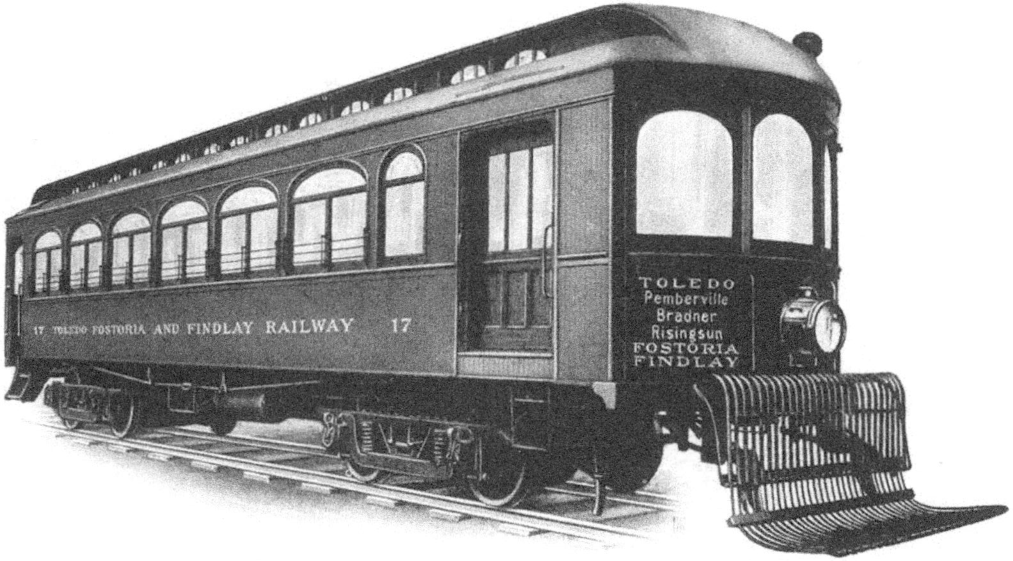

Engraving No. 359.—"Single End" Interurban Combination Passenger and Baggage Car

General Specifications

Length of car body over end plates	40' 3½"	Height, under sills to top of roof	9' 5"
Length of main pass. compartm't	22' 9⅝"	Height, track to top of roof	12' 10"
Length of smoking compartm't	10' 10½"	Distance between bolster centers	27' 6"
Length of baggage room	7' 11½"	Wheel base of trucks	6' 6"
Length of rear vestibule	4' 7⅝"	Seating capacity	45
Length over vestibules	49' 9"	Length of seats	36"
Length over buffers	51' 1"	Width of aisle	19"
Width at sills, including panels	8' 4"	Weight of car body	26,000 lbs.
Width over all	8' 6½"	Weight of trucks	17,500 lbs.

Bottom Frame. Composed of two outside sills each having ⅝" x 7¾" steel plate bolted between yellow pine sills 4½" x 7¾" and 2" x 6"; two center sills of 6" steel I-beams filled with yellow pine and two intermediate sills of 3½" x 6" yellow pine. Tie rods (¾") full width of car with turnbuckle in center at each cross sill.

Trusses. Two under truss rods of 1⅜" round steel, supporting two 6" steel I needle beams and two inside truss bars ½" x 2" on pedestals over bolsters for supporting ends of car.

Floor. Double thickness of ⅞" x 3¼" yellow pine with waterproof building felt between, thoroughly painted and provided with trap doors over motors.

Body. Of alternate single and panel posts with ½" vertical tie rods and sheathed outside with ¾"x2" poplar.

Vestibules. Depressed 6" below car floor at rear end and flush with car floor at front end. All longitudinal sills extend to front buffer, which is same height above rails as at rear end. Single swinging door on each side of rear vestibule and sliding door on each side of front end.

Roof. Monitor deck with steam coach hoods, concealed steel rafter at each panel post, covered with No. 8 duck and fitted with trolley plank whole length.

Windows. Pullman Gothic style fitted with Edwards' sash fixtures, deck sashes hung on Hart's ratchet fixtures.

Glass. All lower side window, door and partition sashes are glazed with polished plate glass. Gothic and deck sashes with opalescent art glass in sections secured in zinc channels.

Interior. Finish of mahogany with principal panels bordered with inlaid colored woods; semi-empire ceiling painted and decorated in color and gold; Pantasote curtains, 11 sectional bronze parcel racks, and bronze trimmings.

Smoking Room. The length of four side windows with swing doors between passenger and baggage compartments.

Baggage Room. At front end with 40" sliding door on each side and iron pipe railing from floor to deck sills to protect motorman from baggage.

Toilet Room. With dry hopper, monolith cement floor and water cooler in alcove on outside.

Seats. Hale & Kilburn No. 10-CE leather seats with 24" head roll stationary backs, bronze grab handles, spring edge cushions and aisle arm rest.

Grab Handles. Hickory, in bronze sockets on posts at each side of steps.

Window Guards. Bronze on end windows and removable three-rod painted iron guards over side windows on outside.

Lighting. Wire and sockets for 35 lamps on separate bases supplied and installed by Car Builder.

Draw Bars. Niles radial spring type with Hovey style of coupler on rear end and rigid steel draw head on front buffer with 6-foot coupling bar on hooks under car.

Track Sanders. Two Nichols-Lintern air type on front end.

Fender. One Providence interurban fender on front end of car.

Fare Register Fixtures. Leather cord with bronze pulleys for register, supplied and attached by Car Builder.

Headlight. One Mosher arc style with wire supplied and installed by Car Builder.

Trolley Retriever. One Knutson No. 2 type on rear end of car.

Heater. One Smith No. 2 hot water heater in front vestibule.

Hand Brake. One malleable ratchet handle with Peacock C drum on front end of car.

Miscellaneous Fittings. Alarm gong, signal bells, Armspear tail lamps, sockets and flags, emergency tools, switch iron and holder are supplied by Car Builder.

Air Brakes. Are supplied and installed by Purchaser or may be installed by Car Builder at shop cost plus 10%.

Electric Power Equipment. (Westinghouse quadruple No. 93-A) supplied and installed by Purchaser at destination or may be installed by Car Builder at shop cost plus 10%.

Trucks. Baldwin, Class 78-25-B with Standard 36" forged-rolled steel wheels with 3" tread on 5½" hammered steel axles, Symington ball center bearings and journal boxes. If cars can be delivered on track on their own wheels the trucks should be attached by Car Builder at car works, otherwise by Purchaser at destination.

If price is wanted on this car, state that it is to be as specified above or name exceptions desired.

Detail drawings and specifications are submitted for Purchaser's approval before starting work.

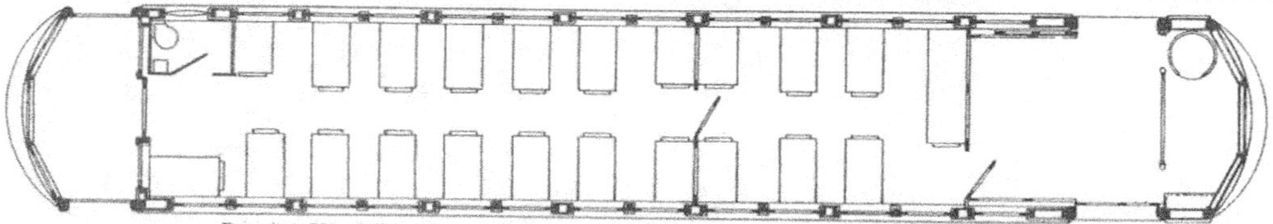

Drawing No. 359.—Plan of "Single End" Combination Passenger and Baggage Car

51. FT. SINGLE END PASSENGER AND SMOKING INTERURBAN CAR

Designed for running with same end forward at all times. Passengers' steps and doors at right side of front vestibule and both sides of rear end. Smoking room at rear end. Main passenger compartment containing toilet and heater cabinet at rear end.

This car is suitable for four 75 H.P. motors, speed of 60 miles per hour, and is one of the most satisfactory types for long interurban railways.

General Specifications and Dimensions

Length of buffers	51' 4"
Length over vestibules	50' 0"
Length of car body	40' 2"
Length of front vestibule	4' 10"
Length of rear vestibule	5' 0"
Width of aisle	12' 0"
Length of smoking room	28' 2"
Width at sills including panels	8' 5½"
Width over all (can be made to suit Purchaser)	8' 8"
Height, under sills to top of roof	9' 5"
Height, track to top of roof	12' 11½"
Distance between bolster centers	28' 2"
Wheel base of trucks	6' 6"
Seating capacity	52
Length of seats	36"
Weight of car body	20½ lbs.
Weight of trucks	26,300 lbs.
Total weight on track ready for service including quadruple Westinghouse No. 304, 90 H.P. motor equipment and air brakes	18,600 lbs.
	32 ton

BOTTOM FRAME. Two outside sills of 4½" x 7¾" and 13¼" x 6" yellow pine with 5⅝" x 7¾" steel plate bolted between (8" steel channel at Purchaser's option). Two center sills of 6" steel I-beams. Two intermediate sills of yellow pine re-enforced at ends with ½" x 6" steel plates. ¾" tie rod with turnbuckle at center at each cross sill, full width of car. Two 10" steel plate truss bolsters. Two 6" I-needle beams. End sill plates ½" x 6" (this car can be made with all-steel bottom frame, steel posts and steel plate truss sheathing below windows).

TRUSSES. Two 1½" under truss rods with 1¾" turnbuckles and two ½" x 2" inside truss bars on pedestals over bolsters for supporting overhanging ends.

FLOOR. Double thickness ⅞" x 3¼" yellow pine with water-proof building felt between.

BODY. Pullman (twin window style with alternate single and panel posts of oak, thoroughly trussed below windows, ½" vertical tie rod at each panel post and sheathed outside with ¾" x 2" poplar.

ROOF. Monitor deck style with steam coach hoods, concealed steel rafter at each panel post, covered with No. 8 canvas, thoroughly painted and fitted with trolley platform over rear truck. (This car can be made with single arch roof having ventilators on top).

VESTIBULES. With floors about 6" below car floor, supported on four 6" steel I-beams, with 8" channel buffers. Each side of rear end and right side of front end are fitted with 31" swing door, double steps with ¼" steel plate treads. Sash in center of front vestibule is stationary, all other vestibule end sashes raise. Front end has 28" door 9" off center toward step. Rear end has 28" door 9" off center toward step. Smoking partition has 28" sliding door in center which allows bulkhead seats to be same length as others and aisle same width full length of car.

INTERIOR FINISH. Polished mahogany in large smooth panels with borders of inlaid lines; semi-empire ceiling in color with gold striping; solid bronze trimmings; thirteen 38" rod bottom parcel racks.

TOILET ROOM. In rear left hand corner, with dry hopper, cement floor, white enamel interior and roof ventilator.

HEATER AND CABINET. Smith No. 2-C hot water heater in asbestos and zinc lined cabinet against toilet room, with 1½" water pipes.

SEATS. Ladies' compartment has 14 Hale & Kilburn's No. 10-C plush seats with stationary head roll backs with grab handles, and 4 corner seats. Smoking room has similar seats in dark green leather. See drawing plan No. 466.

WINDOWS. Single lower side sashes fitted with Edwards' locks with concealed racks, lifts and springs. Thirteen deck sashes have hinges and separate bronze openers; others are stationary. Pantasote curtains on spring rollers with Forsyth fixtures.

GLASS. All body lower sashes glazed with D.S.A. glass. Gothic sashes with etched decorations in center. Chipped glass in deck sashes, toilet and heater cabinet windows. Plate glass in all doors and vestibule end sashes.

WINDOW GUARDS. Body end windows protected by 3 rod bronze guards; lower side windows by 4 rod inside iron guards.

GRAB HANDLES. Hickory in malleable iron sockets, or one piece malleable iron at each side of all steps; also horizontal one piece handle on outside of all vestibule doors.

LIGHTING. Wire, switches, fuses, sockets and lamp brackets for 35 lamps on separate bases and concealed portion of trolley cable, are supplied and installed by Car Builder.

DRAW BARS AND COUPLERS. Niles radial draw bar with Hovey style coupler on each end of car, or heavy steel rigid coupling pocket on each buffer with 6-ft. coupling bar carried on hooks under side of car. Automatic couplers may be supplied at extra charge by Car Builder.

TRACK SANDERS. Two compressed air sanders on front end of car.

FENDER OR PILOT. Supplied by Purchaser and installed by Car Builder.

HEADLIGHT. Supplied by Purchaser. Wiring and bracket for same on front end of car, by Car Builder.

TROLLEY RETRIEVER. Supplied by Purchaser. Wiring and bracket attached by Car Builder.

FARE REGISTER AND FITTINGS. Supplied by Purchaser, and installed by Car Builder.

MISCELLANEOUS FITTINGS. Signal bells with cord and hangers, one 12" alarm gong, emergency tools, switch iron, roof steps, mat and handles, two red lens on rear end, and illuminated sign on front end, are supplied by Purchaser.

PAINTING. Color, lettering, numbers and striping as directed by Purchaser.

HAND BRAKES. Peacock C drum with bronze ratchet windlass on front end of car.

AIR BRAKES. Supplied by Purchaser and may be installed by Car Builder at extra charge for same.

ELECTRIC POWER EQUIPMENT. Supplied and installed by Purchaser at destination, or may be installed by Car Builder at extra charge for same.

TRUCKS. Baldwin Class 78-25-A with Standard 37" forged-rolled steel wheels with rims 3" thick and treads 3" wide on 5½" hammered-steel axles with 4¼" x 8" journals and prepared for Westinghouse No. 304 motors, are supplied by Car Builder. If cars can be delivered on track on their own wheels the bodies should be mounted on trucks at car works; otherwise by Purchaser at destination.

Detail specifications and drawings are submitted for Purchaser's approval before starting work.

Prices can be quoted on duplicates of car as specified above, or with any exceptions desired.

Engraving No. 466—51 Ft. Single End, Two Compartment, Fast Interurban Car.

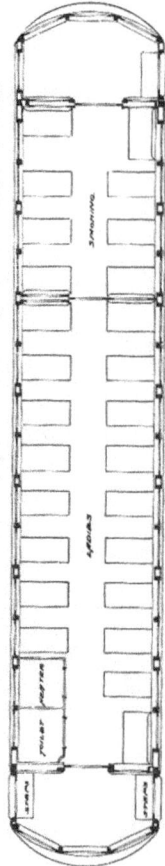

Drawing No. 466—Plan of Single End, Two Compartment Interurban Car with Toilet and Heater Cabinet.

Engraving No. 466—Interior of Two Compartment Interurban Car with Semi-Empire Ceiling.

50 FT. "DOUBLE END" INTERURBAN COMBINATION PASSENGER AND BAGGAGE CAR

With smoking and baggage compartments, convertible motorman's cab in each vestibule, which encloses motorman at front end, allows passenger exit at left side and forms a cabinet for controlling apparatus at rear end, admitting of passenger entrance on both sides, when running with either end forward.

For roads which must use "double end" cars and wish to provide for a limited amount of baggage on each car or at frequent intervals, this is a very convenient type. It also facilitates loading and discharging passengers in city streets and is of proper strength and construction for fast interurban service.

GENERAL SPECIFICATIONS. Same as the passenger and smoking car illustrated and described on opposite page, except that the smoking compartment is reduced to the length of two side windows and a small baggage room is provided with 34" sliding door on each side. Bulkheads protect the step openings. There are four seats with stationary backs against bulkheads in smoking compartment and folding seats in baggage compartment for use of smokers when the room is not filled with baggage, so the average passenger capacity is nearly as great as the exclusive passenger car.

Length of main passenger compartment..........................28' 0"
Length of smoking compartment................................5' 5¾"
Length of baggage room.......................................6' 1¼"

If price is wanted on this car, state that it is to be as specified above or name exceptions desired.

Detail Drawings and specifications are submitted for Purchaser's approval before starting work.

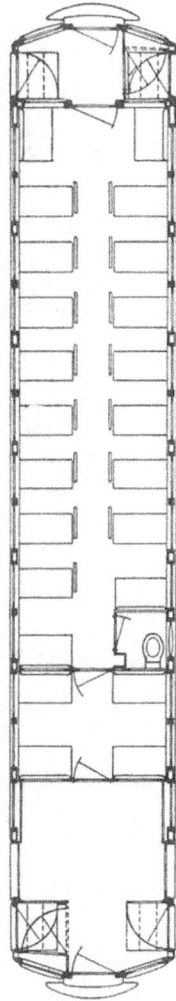

20

Engraving No. 410—"Double End" Combination Passenger and Baggage Interurban Car

Interior of Washington, Baltimore & Annapolis Cars

Drawing No. 410—Plan of "Double End" Combination Passenger, Smoking and Baggage Car

Engraving No. 411.—"Double End" Interurban Passenger and Smoking Car

50 FT. "DOUBLE END" INTERURBAN PASSENGER CAR

With smoking compartment, convertible motorman's cab in each vestibule, which isolates the motorman at front end and encloses controlling apparatus at rear end, at the same time providing steps and entrance for passengers at each side of rear vestibule and left side of front vestibule, when running with either end forward.

This is one of our best plans for roads which must operate "double end" cars. It is very light and strong, has large seating capacity for a car of this size, and is suitable for four 75 H. P. motors and speed of 60 miles per hour, also for convenient handling of passengers on city streets.

General Specifications

Length of car body over end plates	40' 0"	Distance between bolster centers	28' 0"
Length of main passenger compartment	28' 0"	Wheel base of trucks	6' 6"
Length of smoking compartment	11' 6"	Seating capacity	54
Length of toilet room	2'10"	Length of seats	37"
Length of each vestibule	4' 2"	Width of aisle	19½"
Length over vestibules	48' 4"	Weight of car body	28,500 lbs
Length over buffers	50' 0"	Weight of trucks	20,000 lbs
Width at sills including panels	8' 6½"	Weight, complete with quadruple 100 H. P., 1200 V.D.C. electric equipment on track ready for service	78,000 lbs.
Width over all	8' 9"		
Height, under sills to top of roof	9' 4½"		
Height, from track to top of roof	12' 9½"		

Bottom Frame. Composed of two outside sills each having ⅝"x7¾" steel plate bolted between yellow pine sills 4½"x7¾" and 1¾"x6" and four center and intermediate sills of 6" steel I-beams filled with yellow pine; the center sills extending under vestibules from buffer to buffer; ¾" tie rod full width of car with turnbuckle in center at each cross sill. The six longitudinal steel sills are supported on and bolted to six transverse steel beams; viz., two needle beams, two bolsters and two channels under end sills.

Trusses. Two under truss rods of 1⅝" round steel supporting two 6" steel I needle beams and two inside truss bars 2½"x⅜" on pedestals over bolsters for supporting overhanging ends.

Floor. Double thickness of ⅞"x3¼" yellow pine with waterproof building felt between; thoroughly painted and provided with trap doors over motors and entirely covered with Greenwich inlaid linoleum.

Body. Of alternate single and panel posts with ½" vertical tie rods and sheathed outside with ¾"x2" poplar.

Vestibule. At each end flush with car floor, with 27" swing door at each side and in end; convertible motorman's cab at curb side of front end with drop sash in outside door. At rear end the controlling apparatus is enclosed and passengers admitted on both sides. Triple steps at each corner of car, covered with Edwards' self-raising steel trap doors.

Roof. Monitor deck with steam coach hoods, concealed steel rafter at each panel post, covered with 8 oz. duck and fitted at each end with trolley platform supported over deck sills.

Windows. Pullman Gothic style with Edwards' sash locks and rollers. Deck sashes with bronze openers and hinges at ends.

Doors. All of swinging style. Vestibule end doors with drop sash in upper part.

Glass. All lower side windows, doors and partition sashes are glazed with polished plate glass. Gothic and deck sashes with opalescent art glass in zinc channels.

Interior Finish. Selected dark mahogany with marquetry lines of colored woods. Full Empire ceiling in green and gold. Pantasote curtains, 12 bronze parcel racks, and bronze trimmings.

Smoking Room. At one end; 4 windows long, with glazed partition and 23" swinging door.

Toilet Room. With dry hopper, cement floor, white enamel finish and water cooler in alcove on outside.

Seats. Hale & Kilburn No. 199-EE type with bronze grab handles, reversible backs, steel ends and upholstered with dark green leather.

Grab Handles. Hickory in malleable iron sockets at each side of each step; also diagonal handle on outside of each door at same inclination as steps.

Window Guards. Bronze guards on end windows; four-rod painted iron guards hinged at tops at side windows.

Lighting. All material for 30 lamps, conduits, condulets, wire, switches, sockets, brackets and shades, supplied and installed by Contractor for electric equipment, or this may be done by Car Builder at extra charge for same.

Draw Bars and Couplers. Janney automatic M. C. B. radial type with spring buffers for 50 ft. radius curves.

Track Sanders. One Nichols-Lintern air sander on each end of car with flexible hose connection to pipes attached to truck to blow sand under each leading wheel.

Fenders. Supplied and attached by Purchaser at destination, or auxiliary buffers and fenders as shown in engraving may be supplied by Car Builder at extra cost of same.

Headlight. One incandescent-arc style with wiring and brackets on each end.

Trolley Retriever. One on each end of car.

Heater. Electric style, supplied and installed by Purchaser.

Hand Brakes. Fitted with malleable iron Lindstrom lever on each end of car.

Miscellaneous Fittings. Alarm gongs, signal bells, tail lamps, flags and sockets, emergency tools, switch iron and holders, are supplied by Car Builder.

Air Brakes. Supplied by Purchaser and may be installed by Car Builder at shop cost plus 10%.

Electric Power Equipment. General Electric No. 205, 1200 volt D. C., 100 H. P. quadruple motors with double end control, supplied and installed by Purchaser at destination.

Trucks. Baldwin Class 78-25-A with Standard 36" rolled steel wheels, 3" tread, on 5½" axles with 4¼" x 8" journals, fitted with supports for conduit current collecting plow, sander pipes, and Symington ball center and side bearings and journal boxes.

If cars can be delivered on track on their own wheels the trucks should be attached by Car Builder at car works, otherwise by Purchaser at destination.

If price is wanted on this car, state that it is to be as specified above or name exceptions desired.
Detail drawings and specifications are submitted for Purchaser's approval before starting work.

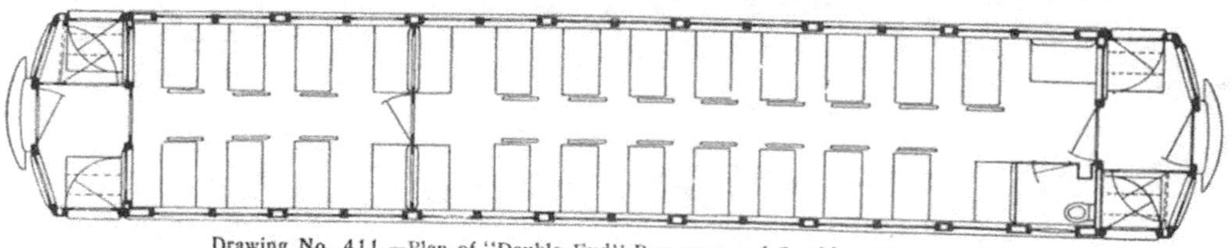

Drawing No. 411.—Plan of "Double End" Passenger and Smoking Interurban Car

Engraving No. 412—"Single End" Interurban Passenger Car

51 FT. "SINGLE END" INTERURBAN PASSENGER CAR

For running with the same end forward at all times, with steps for passengers at each side of rear vestibule and right side of front vestibule, separate motorman's compartment in front vestibule, and with smoking room.

This is one of our best types for transportation of passengers exclusively. Four 75 H. P. motors and speed of 60 miles per hour.

General Specifications

Length of car body over end plates	40′ 2″	Height, track to top of roof	12′ 8½″
Length of passenger compartment	28′ 3″	Distance between bolster centers	28′ 0″
Length of smoking compartment	11′ 11″	Wheel base of trucks	6′ 6″
Length of front vestibule	5′ 0″	Seating capacity	53
Length of rear vestibule	4′ 10″	Length of seats	36″
Length over vestibules	50′ 0″	Width of aisle	20½″
Length over buffers	51′ 4″	Weight of car body	26,700 lbs.
Width at sills including panels	8′ 5½″	Weight of trucks	19,665 lbs.
Width over all	8′ 8″	Weight complete on track ready for service	63,300 lbs.
Height, under sills to top of roof	9′ 5″		

Bottom Frame. Composed of two outside sills each having ⅜″ x 7¾″ steel plate bolted between yellow pine sills 4½″ x 7¾″ and 1¾″ x 6″; two center sills of 6″ steel I-beams filled with yellow pine and two intermediate sills of 3¾″ x 6″ yellow pine; ¾″ tie rod with turnbuckle in center, full width of car at each cross sill.

Trusses. Two under truss rods of suitable diameter supporting two 6″ steel I needle beams and two inside truss bars ⅜″ x 2½″ on pedestals over bolsters for supporting ends of car.

Floor. Double thickness of ⅞″ x 3¼″ yellow pine with waterproof building felt between, thoroughly painted and provided with trap doors over motors.

Body. Of alternate single and panel posts with ½″ vertical rods and sheathed outside with ¾″ x 2″ poplar.

Vestibules. Depressed 6″ below car floor, with 31″ swinging doors and double steps on each side at rear end. Front end has longitudinal partition, isolating motorman from passengers.

Roof. Monitor deck with steam coach hoods, concealed steel rafter at each panel post, covered with No. 8 duck and fitted with trolley plank whole length.

Windows. Pullman twin style with removable storm sashes for lower side windows. Edwards' 13-0 type sash fixtures and 14 ventilator sashes hung on Harts' ratchets.

Glass. All doors and vestibule end sashes have heavy plate glass. Gothic sashes have tinted art glass in three sections with zinc channels. Ventilator sashes have small panes of art glass. Lower side and partition sashes have double strength selected car glass.

Interior. Finish of mahogany with marquetry lines, full empire ceiling of five-ply veneer, painted and decorated. Pantasote curtains; 12 bronze parcel racks and bronze trimmings.

Smoking Room. At front end, four windows long, with swing door to main compartment.

Seats. Hale & Kilburn's No. 10-A seats with 25″ stationary backs, bronze grab handles, upholstered with green plush and leather in smoking compartment.

Window Guards. Bronze on end windows and removable three-rod painted iron guards over outside windows.

Grab Handles. Hickory, in malleable iron sockets at each side of steps and horizontal bronze on vestibule doors.

Toilet Room. With dry hopper, floor of monolith cement, white enamel inside finish and water cooler in alcove on outside.

Lighting. Wire, fuses, switches, cabinets, sockets, 3 holophane hemispheres and "goose neck" brackets for 35 lamps, also trolley cable supplied and installed by Car Builder.

Draw Bars. Niles radial spring type with Hovey style of coupler on each end of car.

Track Sanders. Two Nichols-Lintern air style on front end of car.

Fender. One Detroit "apron" style fender on front end of car.

Headlight. One luminous-arc style on front vestibule.

Trolley Retriever. One Knutson No. 2 on rear vestibule.

Heater. One Smith No. 2 hot water heater in front vestibule.

Hand Brake. With malleable ratchet handle in front vestibule.

Miscellaneous Fittings. Alarm gong, signal bells, electric bells with push buttons, tail lamps, sockets and flags, emergency tools, switch iron and holders, cuspidors for smoking room, and cocoa aisle mat for main compartment, are supplied by Car Builder.

Air Brakes. Are supplied by Purchaser and may be installed by Car Builder at shop cost plus 10%.

Electric Power Equipment. (Westinghouse quadruple No. 112-B) supplied and installed by Purchaser at destination or installation may be made by Car Builder at shop cost plus 10%.

Trucks. Baldwin Class 78-25-A with Standard forged-rolled steel wheels, 36″ diameter, rims $4\frac{3}{16}$″ wide x 2½″ thick, on A. S. & I. R. A. 5½″ hammered steel axles, Symington ball center bearings and journal boxes.

If cars can be delivered on track on their own wheels, the trucks should be attached by Car Builder at car works, otherwise by Purchaser at destination.

If price is wanted on this car, state that it is to be as specified above or name exceptions desired.

Detail drawings and specifications are submitted for Purchaser's approval before starting work.

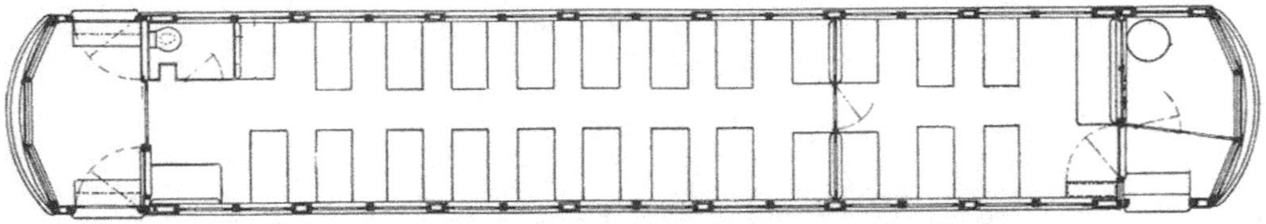

Drawing No. 412—Plan of "Single End" Interurban Passenger and Smoking Car

Engraving No. 435—39 Ft. Double Truck "Double End" City Service Car

28 FT. BODY, DOUBLE TRUCK, DOUBLE END CAR

For city and suburban service with either end forward. It can be used either for platform prepayment or inside collection of fares. When used as a "Pay-Enter" car it is fitted with iron railings extending from center of steps at curb side of rear end and devil strip side of front end to center of end bulkhead doors.

General Specifications

Length of car body over end plates	28′ 0″	Height, from track to top of roof	11′ 8″
Length over vestibules	38′ 2″	Distance between bolster centers	16′ 0″
Length over buffers	39′ 4″	Wheel base of trucks	5′ 0″
Length of each vestibule	5′ 1″	Seating capacity	42
Width over sheathing at sills	7′ 10¼″	Weight of car body, about	15,000 lbs.
Width over all	8′ 0″	Weight of trucks (2) about	12,000 lbs.
Height, under sills to top of roof	8′ 10″		

BOTTOM FRAME. Two side sills of 4¾″x 7⅝″ and 1¾″x6″ yellow pine with ½″x7″ steel plate bolted between. Two center sills of 6″ steel I-beams filled with yellow pine. End sills of 4¾″x7⅝″ oak with ½″x4½″ steel plate. ¾″ tie rod with turnbuckle in center at each cross sill. Bolsters 8″ steel plate truss style.

FLOOR. Of ⅞″x3¼″ yellow pine with hard maple floor strips in aisle between seats. Trap doors over motors.

TRUSSES. 1¼″ under truss rods with turnbuckle supporting one 6″ I needle beam in center. Inside truss bars ⅜″x2½″ supported over bolsters. Inside truss planks 2″x10″.

BODY. Single side posts of oak or ash; "W" style bracing; sheathed on outside with vertical ½″x2″ poplar.

ROOF. Monitor deck style with steam coach style of hoods over vestibules. ⅜″x1½″ steel carline at each side post. Covered with No. 8 canvas, thoroughly painted and fitted with trolley platform whole length.

VESTIBULES. At each end, 9″ below car floor, 37″ step with malleable iron ends and Universal safety treads at each side. Platform sills reinforced with two ½″x3″x4″ steel angles and two ½″x5″ steel plates. Buffers sheathed with ½″x6″ steel plates full width.

DOORS. Double independent sliding doors with 38″ opening in each end of car body. Double folding doors with 33″ opening at each side of each vestibule.

WINDOWS. Nine windows in each side of car body. Upper sashes stationary. Lower sashes drop with hinged covers over openings. Three single drop sash windows in end of each vestibule. Nine deck sashes on each side of roof; three stationary and six hinged at ends and operated with double bronze deck sash openers.

GLASS. Double strength selected car glass in all lower sashes and doors, rippled cathedral or clear glass in upper side sashes. Woven wire glass in deck sashes.

CURTAINS. Pantasote on spring rollers on all windows and doors in car body.

INTERIOR FINISH. All interior panels, mouldings, doors, sashes, etc., of mahogany in smooth, sanitary finish, varnished and polished. Ceiling of three-ply veneer, varnished or painted and decorated.

SEATS. Of spring rattan in two sections on each side, longitudinal with backs against walls of car and panelled underneath.

TRIMMINGS. For doors, sashes, bell cords, etc., of polished solid bronze.

HAND STRAPS. Plain leather, 13″ long, 16 on each side, on mahogany rails supported on bronze combination bell cord, register rod and hand rail brackets.

REGISTERS. Supplied and attached by Purchaser. Rod with leather pulls along one side of car supplied and installed by Car Builder.

Interior of No. 435 Double Truck "Double End" City Car

LIGHTING. Material for 25 lamps on separate bases and concealed portion of trolley cable supplied and installed by Car Builder.

GRAB HANDLES. On each side of each vestibule side door of 30″ hickory in malleable iron sockets.

WINDOW GUARDS. Three-rod bronze guards on outside of each body end window. Four-rod painted iron removable guards on outside of all side windows.

HEATERS. Twelve panel style electric heaters and all material supplied by Purchaser and installed by Car Builder, or supplied by Car Builder at extra charge for same.

DRAW BARS. Rigid steel draw head bolted to each buffer and long coupling bar carried on hooks under side of car.

TRACK SANDERS. One Nichols-Lintern air style on each end of car.

FENDERS. On each end of car, supplied by Purchaser and attached by Car Builder.

HEADLIGHT. Supplied by Purchaser. Wiring for same at each end of car by Car Builder.

TROLLEY CATCHER. Supplied and attached by Purchaser.

MISCELLANEOUS FITTINGS. Alarm gongs, signal bells, roof steps, handles and mats, switch iron and holders, are supplied by Car Builder.

HAND BRAKES. In each vestibule, 12″ bronze ratchet handle with Ackley brake under platform.

AIR BRAKES. Supplied and installed by Purchaser at destination, or installation may be made by Car Builder at extra charge for same.

ELECTRIC POWER EQUIPMENT. Supplied and installed by Purchaser at destination, or installation may be made by Car Builder at extra charge for same.

TRUCKS. Supplied and attached by Purchaser at destination, or by Car Builder at extra charge for same.

Price can be quoted on duplicates of this car as specified above or with any exceptions desired.

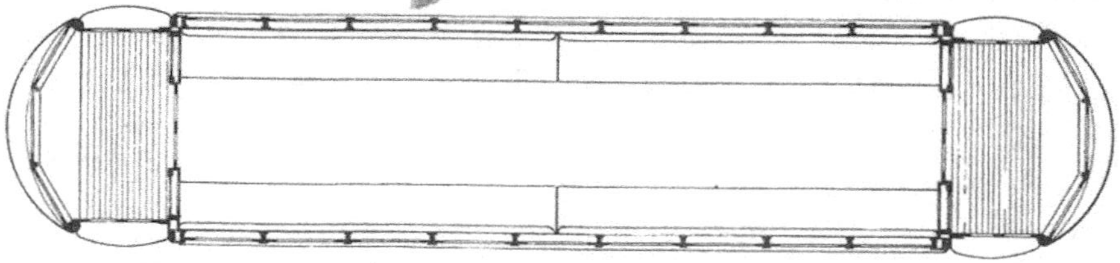

Drawing No. 435—Plan of 39 Ft. (28 Ft. Body) "Double End" City Service Car

Engraving No. 444—32 Ft. Single Truck "Double End" Pay-As-You-Enter City Car

BODY. All posts of ash or oak; ⅞" inside truss rods with turnbuckle in center; vertical outside sheathing of ¾"x2" poplar. Double sash windows, upper sashes stationary, lower ones to drop, with hinged covers over sash pockets. End bulkheads with panel in center and door at each side.

ROOF. Monitor deck style with detachable hoods; ½" steel carline at each side post, covered with ½" poplar and No. 8 canvas and thoroughly painted. Trolley platform whole length of car body. Eight deck sashes on each side, four fitted with double sash openers and four stationary.

VESTIBULES. At each end of car with three drop sashes across ends, double folding doors at curb side of rear end, single door, under control of motorman, sliding toward car body between double panels and sashes at opposite side. An iron pipe railing, as shown in drawing, separates entrance from exit. Vestibule floors 9" below car floor.

INTERIOR FINISH. Quartered oak in smooth, sanitary finish. Ceiling of three-ply veneer or composition board, painted and with advertising mouldings, polished bronze trimming.

GLASS. Heavy plate in doors; selected sheet glass in windows; wire glass in deck sashes.

CURTAINS. Car body windows and end doors fitted with Pantasote curtains on spring rollers.

SEATS. Eight Hale & Kilburn's No. 98-A spring rattan seats with reversible backs and bronze grab handles, and four longitudinal seats as shown in drawing.

LIGHTING. Material for 15 lamps on separate bases and concealed portion of trolley cable are supplied and installed by Car Builder, also a cable box, lined with asbestos, along each side of car under seats.

HAND STRAPS. 16 per car, located over longitudinal seats, of plain leather 16" long.

WINDOW GUARDS. Body end windows, fitted with three rod bronze guards.

GRAB HANDLES. At each side of each step, of hickory in bronze sockets.

DRAW BARS. Rigid coupling pocket bolted to each buffer and coupling bar 1¼"x3"x5¼" carried on hooks under side of car.

TRACK SANDERS. One at each end of car under corner seat, operated by foot button in vestibule.

FENDERS. Supplied and attached by Purchaser.

FARE REGISTER OR FARE BOX. Supplied by Purchaser.

HEADLIGHT. Supplied by Purchaser; wiring supplied and installed at each end of car by Car Builder.

TROLLEY CATCHER. Supplied by Purchaser.

HEATERS. Electric style, one under each seat with switches and fuses, supplied and installed by Car Builder.

MISCELLANEOUS. Alarm gongs, signal bells, roof steps, mats and handles, supplied by Car Builder.

HAND BRAKES. In each vestibule, one vertical geared malleable iron brake wheel with staff, ratchet and chain.

AIR BRAKES. Supplied and installed by Purchaser, or by Car Builder at extra charge for same.

TRUCKS. Supplied and attached by Purchaser at destination, or by Car Builder at extra charge for same.

ELECTRIC POWER EQUIPMENT. Supplied and installed by Purchaser at destination, or installation may be made by Car Builder at extra charge for same.

ROYALTY. On Pay-As-You-Enter patents to be paid by the Railway Company.

Price can be quoted on duplicates of this car as specified above or with any exceptions desired.

Interior of No. 444 Single Truck Pay-As-You-Enter Car

SINGLE TRUCK, DOUBLE END, PAY-AS-YOU-ENTER CAR

Prepayment cars for City service seem to have passed the experimental stage. The advantages from increased revenue, decreased accidents and greater mileage from cars, have been demonstrated. Engravings and drawing No. 444 show one of the best styles of P. A. Y. E. cars. The space behind railing in front vestibule can be used for smoking.

General Specifications

Length of car body over end plates .... 20' 8"
Length over vestibules .... 30' 9"
Length over buffers .... 32' 2"
Length of vestibules .... 5' 1½"
Width at sills, including panels .... 8' 1¼"
Width over all .... 8' 5¼"
Height, under sills to top of roof ..... 9' 0"
Height, from track to top of roof ...... 11' 2½"
Seating capacity 24
Length of cross seats .... 33"
Width of aisle .... 21½"
Wheel base of truck .... 7' 6"
Weight of car body, about .... 12,000 lbs.
Weight of truck, about .... 5,000 lbs.

BOTTOM FRAME. Side sills of yellow pine, 4¾"x8". End sills of oak, 5½"x8". Truck frame sills, 3¾"x6". Trap doors for Westinghouse No. 68 motors. FLOOR. Of ⅞"x3¼" yellow pine, lengthwise of car, double under seats, single with maple floor strips in aisle.

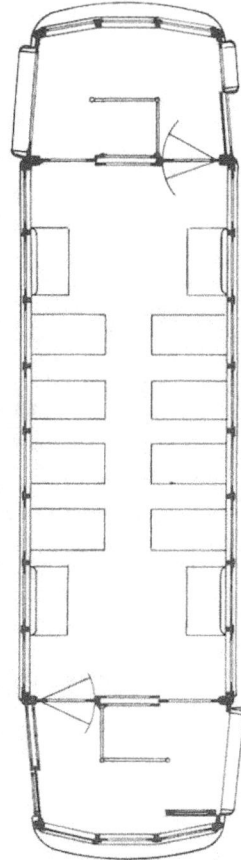

Drawing No. 444—Plan of Single Truck "Double End" Pay-As-You-Enter Car

24

Interior of No. 463 "Single End" Pay-As-You-Enter Car

DOUBLE TRUCK, SINGLE END PAY-AS-YOU-ENTER CAR

For use with same end forward at all times. The motorman is isolated from passengers but has control of the front exit door. The conductor controls rear entrance door with a foot lever. It has large and conveniently arranged standing room for rush hours, also ample seating capacity for average loads. This style is recommended for heavy traffic and where local conditions permit running "single ended."

General Specifications

Length of car body over end plates	31' 3"	Height, from track to top of roof	11' 10⅜"
Length of front vestibule over buffers	5' 2"	Length of seats	33"
Length of front vestibule inside	4' 4"	Width of aisle	21"
Length of rear vestibule over buffer	5' 10'	Seating capacity, about	45
Length over buffers	42' 3"	Distance between bolster centers	18' 11"
Width over all	8' 3½"	Wheel base of trucks	5' 0"
Width inside	7' 3"	Weight of car body, about	16,000 lbs.
Height, under sills to top of roof	9' 0⅜"	Weight of trucks, about	12,000 lbs.

BOTTOM FRAME. Side sills of 4"x7¾" and 1¾"x5¾" yellow pine with ⅜"x12" steel plate bolted between. Two center sills, 3½"x4½" yellow pine. End sills, 4¾"x10⅞" oak. Cross sills, 2½"x5¼" oak with tie rods. Trap doors over motors. . Bolsters, 9" steel plate truss type.

FLOOR. Double, of 1 3/16"x3¼" yellow pine with 1" of mineral wool between and hard maple strips screwed to floor in aisles.

BODY. Single side posts of ash or oak. Concave and convex panels below side windows. Inside truss bars, ⅜"x2½" supported over bolsters. Front end bulkhead at left side with 30" sliding door at right side next to front exit step. Rear end bulkhead with double panels in center and 28" sliding door at each side, both sliding toward center of car.

ROOF. Monitor deck style with detachable hoods over vestibules. Steel carline, ⅝"x1½" at each side post. Covered with 7/16" poplar, No. 6 canvas thoroughly painted, and fitted with trolley platform over rear truck.

VESTIBULES. Motorman's compartment with three single drop sashes across front, closed with panel and sashes at left side and separated at right side from front exit by a partition with 21" swing door. 35" step with safety tread at front end. Conductor's P-A-Y-E rear vestibule with three single drop sashes across end.

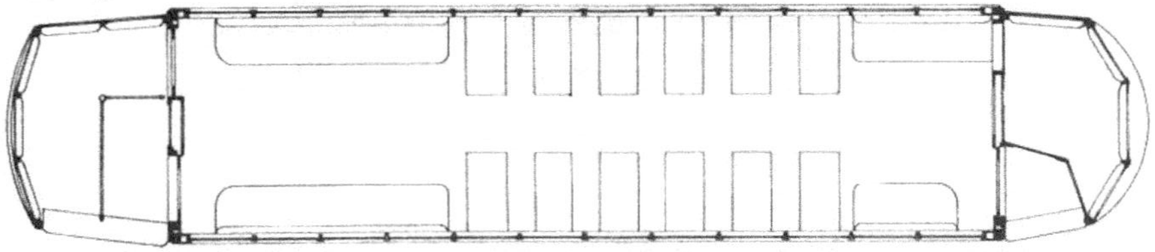

Drawing No. 463—Plan of 42 Ft. Double Truck "Single End" Pay-As-You-Enter City Car

Engraving No. 463—Double Truck "Single End" Pay-As-You-Enter Car

Closed with panels and two sashes on devil strip side; open with 4' 6¼" step covered with safety tread at curb side and with 1¼" iron pipe railing separating entrance from exit as shown in plan. Platform sills reinforced with two steel angles 7"x3½"x½" and two steel angles 5"x4"x½". Buffers sheathed with ⅜"x7" steel plates full width.

DOORS. Entrance door in rear bulkhead controlled by conductor with foot lever attached to center panel. Exit door at front end controlled by motorman with overhead lever above center window.

WINDOWS. Twelve windows in each side of car body. Upper sashes stationary. Lower sashes drop into pockets which are covered when sashes are up or down. Three windows in devil strip side of vestibules of same style as body windows. Twelve deck sashes on each side of car, alternate ones being hinged at front ends and operated with bronze deck sash openers.

GLASS. All windows glazed with double strength selected sheet glass. Deck sashes with chipped imitation bevel edge glass. All doors with heavy plate glass.

CURTAINS. All side and front end body windows and window and door in motorman's partition are fitted with Pantasote curtains on spring rollers.

INTERIOR FINISH. Panels, doors, sashes, mouldings, etc., of quartered oak of plain, smooth finish in natural color. Bevel edge mirror in heater panel at left side of front bulkhead. Ceiling of three-ply veneer decorated and varnished and fitted with advertising mouldings.

SEATS. Twelve Hale & Kilburn's No. 11-A stationary back spring rattan cross seats with bronze grab handles, steel pedestals and 18" backs; also four longitudinal seats on cast iron pedestals in corners of car, as shown in drawing No. 463. All cushions have spring edge.

TRIMMINGS. For doors, sashes, bell cords, etc., of solid polished bronze.

HAND STRAPS. Over longitudinal seats only, of plain riveted leather on oak rails in bronze sockets.

REGISTER OR FARE BOX. Supplied and installed by Purchaser.

LIGHTING. Wiring and material for 25 lamps on separate bases, concealed portion of trolley cable and cable boxes along truss planks, are supplied and installed by Car Builder.

GRAB HANDLES. Each side of each step fitted with hickory grab handle in bronze sockets. Horizontal bronze grab handle on motorman's partition at front exit.

WINDOW GUARDS. Of three rod polished bronze on both sides of end bulkhead windows and inside on motorman's door. Single rod across two side windows of rear vestibule.

HEATERS. Smith forced down draft hot air type, supplied by Purchaser and installed by Car Builder in front vestibule with asbestos and tin-lined duct with grill openings along truss plank on left side of car.

DRAW BARS. Rigid coupling pocket bolted to each buffer and coupling bar 1¾"x5' 3½" carried on hooks under side of car.

TRACK SANDERS. Two mechanical sanders under front end of car with controlling lever in front vestibule.

FENDERS. Supplied and attached by Purchaser or by Car Builder at extra charge for same.

HEADLIGHT. Front end of roof fitted with Dayton No. 585 incandescent headlight. Front center vestibule panel fitted with sockets and wiring for arc headlight which will be supplied by Purchaser.

TROLLEY CATCHER. Supplied by Purchaser and attached by Car Builder.

PAINTING. As directed by Purchaser.

MISCELLANEOUS FITTINGS. Alarm gong, signal bells, roof steps, handles and mat and electric bells with push buttons on each side post, are supplied by Car Builder.

HAND BRAKES. In front vestibule with 15" horizontal iron wheel and Peacock drum under platform.

AIR BRAKES. Supplied and installed by Purchaser, or installed by Car Builder at extra charge for same.

ELECTRIC POWER EQUIPMENT. Supplied and installed by Purchaser, or installed by Car Builder at extra charge for same.

TRUCKS. Supplied and attached by Purchaser at destination, or by Car Builder at extra charge for same.

ROYALTY OR LICENSE. On Pay-As-You-Enter patents to be paid by the Railway Company.

Price can be quoted on duplicates of this car as specified above or with any exceptions desired.

Engraving No. 439—55 Ft. Oklahoma Type Interurban Car with Observation Vestibule

55 FT. SINGLE END, COMBINATION BAGGAGE, PASSENGER AND OBSERVATION INTERURBAN CAR

This plan provides a large main passenger compartment with toilet room in center of car, baggage room with folding seats for smokers, separate motorman's cab at front end and an observation-smoking compartment with large windows at rear end.

It includes practically all the accommodations of a steam railroad train of baggage, coach and observation cars, and is recommended for long runs and limited service.

General Specifications and Dimensions

Length over buffers	54' 7"	Height, from track to top of roof	12' 11¾"
Length over vestibules	53' 11"	Distance between bolster centers	32' 11"
Length of main compartment	34' 5"	Wheel base of trucks	6' 4"
Length of observation compartment	10' 2"	Seating capacity	58
Length of baggage room	8' 3"	Length of seats	41"
Width over sheathing at sills	9' 6"	Width of aisle	22"
Width over all	9' 8½"	Weight of car body	30,000 lbs.
Height, under sills to top of roof	9' 6¾"	Weight of trucks	19,000 lbs.

Bottom Frame. Two outside sills of 4½"x7¾" and 1¾"x6" yellow pine with ⅝"x7¾" steel plate bolted between. Four center and intermediate sills of 6" steel I-beams between yellow pine fillers extending from buffer to buffer; supported on and bolted to 10" plate bolsters, 6" needle I-beams and fitted with ¾" tie rods having turnbuckles in center at each cross sill.

Trusses. Two 1⅝" under truss rods with 1¾" turnbuckles and two ⅜"x2½" inside truss bars on pedestals over bolsters for supporting overhanging ends.

Floor. Double thickness of ⅞"x3¼" yellow pine with waterproof building felt between and covered with corrugated rubber mat in rear vestibule.

Body. Pullman style twin Gothic windows with alternate single posts and panel piers, thoroughly braced, sheathed with ¾"x2" poplar continuous from sills to letter panels and with ½" vertical tie rod at each post.

Roof. Monitor deck style with steam coach hoods, concealed steel carline at each panel post, covered with No. 8 duck, painted and fitted with trolley platform full length.

Motorman's Cab. In center at front end with swinging door in rear; with glass on all sides and fitted with curtains to exclude light. Heavy iron pipe railing from floor to roof to protect motorman from baggage, may be used instead of enclosed cab.

Baggage Room. At front end with 42" sliding door on each side. When not filled with baggage, smoking may be permitted in this room.

Observation Vestibule. At rear end with 30" double folding door, triple steps with safety treads and Edwards' self-raising steel trap door at each side. 26" swing door in center of rear end and front bulkhead. In warm weather the large windows surrounding this vestibule are removed, making it practically open but protected by bronze grills and drop guard rails at steps. In cold weather the observation feature is retained but protected by large plate glass windows. Smoking may be permitted.

Interior Finish. In main compartment, of selected mahogany with large smooth panels having marquetry line borders. Window heads of same curvature as on outside. Solid bronze trimmings, sectional rod bottom parcel racks and Empire ceiling. In observation room, of dark Flemish oak in dull finish. In baggage room, of golden oak in gloss finish.

Toilet Room. In rear left-hand corner of passenger compartment with dry hopper, white enamel finish, cement floor, roof ventilator and water cooler in alcove on outside.

Seats. Nineteen Hale & Kilburn No. 110 C. E. seats with stationary 25" backs, bronze grab handle, spring edge cushions and upholstered with dark green leather. Three cross bulkhead seats, one longitudinal corner seat in main compartment and folding wooden seats in baggage room are supplied and installed by Car Builder. Loose parlor chairs and folding camp chairs for observation vestibule are selected and furnished by Purchaser, or by Car Builder at extra charge for same.

Windows. Single lower sashes fitted with Edwards' locks with concealed racks, to raise between double Gothic sashes. Deck sashes in three sections; the center ones hung on Hart's ratchet fixtures. Pantasote curtains on spring rollers below Gothic sashes.

Interior of No. 439 Combination Interurban Car

Glass. Polished plate in lower side and end windows, partitions and doors. Rippled Cathedral glass in coppered channels in Gothic, toilet room and deck sashes.

Lighting. Wire, switches, fuses, sockets and lamp brackets for 35 lamps on separate bases located on side posts, one over each seat and concealed portion of trolley cable are supplied and installed by Car Builder.

Draw Bars and Couplers. On each end, automatic M. C. B. radial type.

Track Sanders. Two Nichols-Lintern compressed air style on front end.

Pilot. One locomotive style under front end.

Headlight. Supplied by Purchaser. Wiring and brackets for same on front end by Car Builder.

Trolley Retriever. One Knutson No. 2 on rear end of car.

Heater. Hot water style, located in baggage room with pipes extending through main compartment and observation vestibule.

Fare Register and Fittings. Supplied by Purchaser, or by Car Builder at extra charge for same.

Miscellaneous Fittings. Signal bells with cord and hangers, alarm gongs, emergency tools, switch iron, cuspidors, roof steps, mats and handles, hickory grab handles in bronze sockets, oil tail lamps and flags, are supplied by Car Builder.

Hand Brakes. In front end with malleable iron Lindstrom handle.

Air Brakes. Supplied and installed by Purchaser at destination, or installed by Car Builder at extra charge for same.

Electric Power Equipment. Supplied and installed by Purchaser at destination, or may be installed by Car Builder at extra charge for same.

Trucks. Supplied and attached by Purchaser at destination, or by Car Builder at extra charge for same. If cars can be delivered on track on their own wheels, the trucks should be supplied and attached by Car Builder at car works.

Prices can be quoted on duplicates of car as specified above or with any exceptions desired.

Detail specifications and drawings are submitted for Purchaser's approval before starting work.

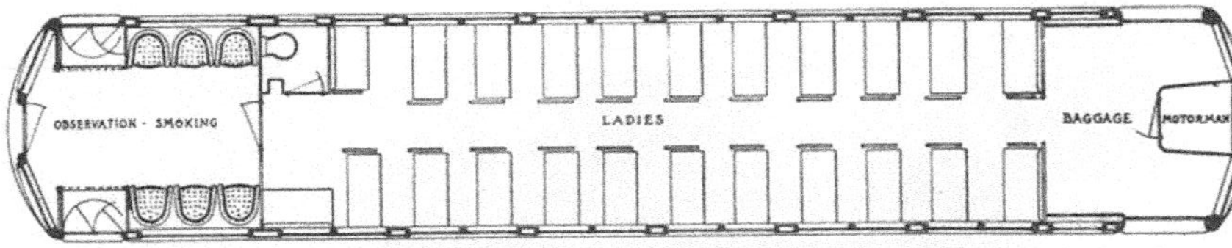

Drawing No. 439—Plan of Oklahoma Type Combination Baggage, Passenger and Observation Car

Engraving No. 423—"Double End" Combination Passenger, Smoking and Baggage Car

48 FT. "DOUBLE END" THREE COMPARTMENT PASSENGER, SMOKING AND BAGGAGE CAR

With passenger entrance at curb side of rear vestibule and opposite side of front vestibule when running with either end forward.

It has toilet room, hot water heater, electric cabinet, folding seats in baggage room and is a very good design for general interurban traffic over hilly country and long, fast runs where baggage, express and package freight is carried, and most of the traffic is from terminal points.

GENERAL SPECIFICATIONS. Are same as the exclusive passenger car on opposite page, except as follows:

BAGGAGE ROOM. At one end of car, occupying the length of three side windows, with sliding door on each side, folding seats for smokers when not filled with baggage, and finished in oak.

SMOKING ROOM. Located next to baggage room, occupying the length of three side windows, with swing door in each bulkhead and furnished with six reversible back seats same as in passenger car.

MAIN PASSENGER COMPARTMENT. Occupying the length of seven side windows and furnished with eleven reversible and two stationary back seats.

SEATING CAPACITY. 46 persons.

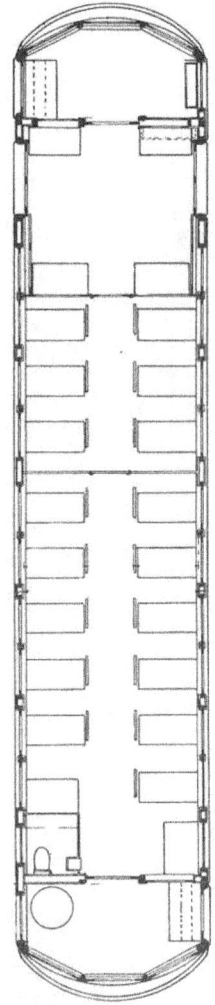

Drawing No. 423—Plan of "Double End" Combination Passenger, Smoking and Baggage Car

Interior of "Double End" Interurban Cars

Engraving No. 460—"Single End" Two Compartment Light Interurban Car

Interior of "Single End" Light Interurban Car

47 FT. "SINGLE END" TWO COMPARTMENT LIGHT INTERURBAN CAR

This car is especially designed to resemble city cars as much as possible and at the same time to afford all the comforts and conveniences necessary for long runs and fast speed. It is particularly desirable in localities where a prejudice exists against the use of city streets by large interurban cars and for local interurban traffic.

General Specifications

Length over buffers	46' 4"	Width over all	8' 6"	Length of seats	34½"
Length of car body	36' 2"	Height, under sills to top of roof	9' 7"	Width of aisle	22"
Length of front vestibule	4' 6"	Height, track to top of roof	13' 1"	Weight of car body	23,800 lbs.
Length of rear platform	5' 1"	Distance betw'n bolster centers	23' 2"	Weight of trucks	16,500 lbs.
Length of smoking compartm't	11' 5"	Wheel base of trucks	6' 6"	Weight on track, complete with quadruple Westinghouse No. 310-C equipm'ts	55,735 lbs
Length of main pass. compart't	24' 9"	Seating capacity	45		
Width at sills, includ'g sheath'g	8' 4"				

Bottom Frame. Two outside sills of 4" x 8¾" yellow pine, reinforced inside with ½" x 12" steel plate. Two center sills of yellow pine. Cross sills of oak. Cable conduit between center sills.

Trusses. Inside truss bars ⅞" x 2½" on iron pedestals over bolsters for supporting overhanging ends.

Floor. Of ⅞" x 3¼" yellow pine, double thickness with waterproof tarred felt paper between. Eight small trap doors over commutators and bearings.

Body. Curved panels below windows, single posts of 1¾" sweep. Thirteen two-sash windows on each side. Outside panels of poplar.

Roof. Monitor deck style with detachable hoods, covered with No. 6 duck and fitted with trolley platform at rear end.

Vestibule. At front end with partition at right side, separating motorman from step opening and enclosed at left side. Open rear platform with No. 14 steel dasher, single step at each side and Woods' folding gate at left side. Steps fitted with Universal safety treads.

Smoking Room. The length of four side windows at front end with 32" sliding door in right-hand front corner and 24" swing door in rear partition.

Toilet Room. In rear left-hand corner, with dry hopper. No. 16 sheet steel floor, ventilator in roof and water cooler in alcove on outside.

Windows. Stationary upper sashes with curved heads, lower sashes fitted with locks, lifts and springs and to raise. Stationary storm sashes on all side and vestibule windows fastened at top, center and bottom. One-half of deck sashes are hinged at front end with bronze opener at rear end, other half are stationary.

Curtains. Pantasote, on spring rollers with Forsyth ring fixtures.

Doors. 1⅜" thick, 32" sliding door in front end; 40" door in rear end. Swing door in vestibule, toilet, heater cabinet and smoking partition. Blount door check on smoking room door.

Glass. Polished plate in windows, doors and bulkheads. White chipped, imitation bevel edge in deck sashes. D. T. A. selected car glass in storm sashes.

Interior Finish. Of quarter-sawed oak in natural color, smooth, sanitary finish of panels and mouldings. Monitor deck ceiling of three-ply veneer. Bronze trimmings and continuous bronze parcel racks along each side of car.

Seats. Hale & Kilburn's No. 10-A type with stationary backs, bronze grab handle and upholstered with plush; 54¼" seat against front bulkhead in smoker, four seats with back against smoking partition and one against heater room.

Grab Handles. Hickory, in bronze sockets at each side of steps; also horizontal handle on vestibule partition.

Window Guards. On left side of car only; of painted iron hinged at tops for cleaning glass. Inside guards of bronze.

Lighting. Material for 30 lamps, electric bells complete and concealed part of trolley cable, supplied and installed by Car Builder.

Draw Bars and Couplers. Rigid coupling pocket bolted to each buffer and five-foot coupling bar carried on hooks under side of car.

Track Sanders. Two lever controlled sanders on front end of car.

Fenders. One Detroit interurban style on front end of car, supplied and attached by Purchaser.

Trolley Retriever. Supplied and attached by Purchaser.

Heater. Smith No. 1-C hot water type in an asbestos and zinc lined cabinet next to toilet room, supplied and installed complete by Car Builder.

Hand Brakes. In front vestibule; 17" horizontal wheel with Peacock C drum.

Miscellaneous Fittings. Signal bells, alarm gong, roof steps, handle, mat, headlight and tail lamp sockets and coal box are supplied by Car Builder.

Register Rods. ⅝" square rod with leather pulls on bronze brackets along each side of car.

Air Brakes. Supplied and installed by Purchaser at destination, or installed by Car Builder at extra charge for same.

Electric Power Equipment. Supplied and installed by Purchaser at destination, or installed by Car Builder at extra charge for same.

Trucks. Baldwin Class 78-22-A with Standard 33" rolled steel wheels with 3" tread and 2½" rims, on 5" hammered steel axles with 4¼" x 8" journals, and fitted for Westinghouse No. 310-C motors, are supplied by Car Builder and attached by Purchaser at destination, or attached by Car Builder if cars can be delivered on their own wheels.

Price can be quoted on duplicates of car as specified above, or with any exceptions desired.
Detail specifications and drawings are prepared for Purchaser's approval before starting work.

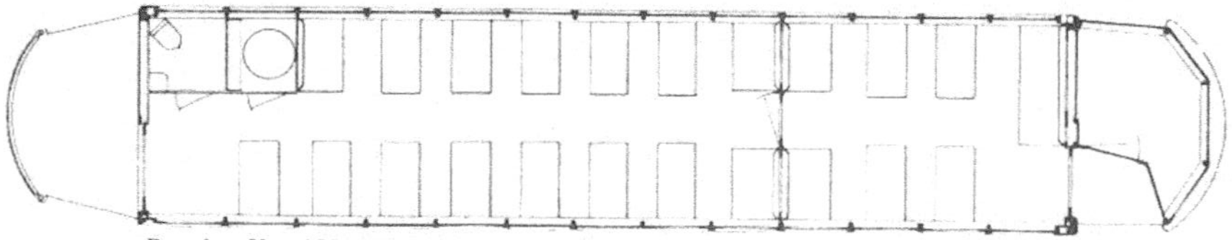

Drawing No. 460—Plan of "Single End" Two Compartment Light Interurban Car

Engraving No. 423 "Double End" Combination Passenger, Smoking and Baggage Car

48 FT. "DOUBLE END" THREE COMPARTMENT PASSENGER, SMOKING AND BAGGAGE CAR

With passenger entrance at curb side of rear vestibule and opposite side of front vestibule when running with either end forward.

It has toilet room, hot water heater, electric cabinet, folding seats in baggage room and is a very good design for general interurban traffic over hilly country and long, fast runs where baggage, express and package freight is carried, and most of the traffic is from terminal points.

GENERAL SPECIFICATIONS. Are same as the exclusive passenger car on opposite page, except as follows:

BAGGAGE ROOM. At one end of car, occupying the length of three side windows, with sliding door on each side, folding seats for smokers when not filled with baggage, and finished in oak.

SMOKING ROOM. Located next to baggage room, occupying the length of three side windows, with swing door in each bulkhead and furnished with six reversible back seats same as in passenger car.

MAIN PASSENGER COMPARTMENT. Occupying the length of seven side windows and furnished with eleven reversible and two stationary back seats.

SEATING CAPACITY. 46 persons.

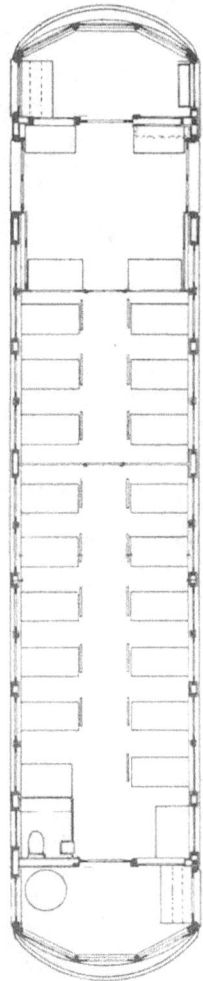

Drawing No. 423 Plan of "Double End" Combination Passenger, Smoking and Baggage Car

Interior of "Double End" Interurban Cars

29

Engraving No. 377—"Double End" Interurban Trailer Car

48 FT. SINGLE COMPARTMENT "DOUBLE END" INTERURBAN TRAILER CAR

This is a light, strong, inexpensive and handsome car with large seating capacity and suitable for as fast speed as electric cars make when pulling trailers.

A few extra cars of this kind for excursions, special parties and emergency calls to move large crowds, are proving profitable investments on many interurban roads.

General Specifications

Length over buffers	47' 10"
Length over vestibules	46' 6"
Length of car body	36' 6"
Length of vestibules	5' 0"
Width at sills, includ'g sheathing	8' 5"
Width over all	8' 7½"
Height, under sills to top of roof	9' 6"
Height, from track to top of roof	12' 9½"
Distance between bolster centers	25' 10"
Wheel base of trucks	5' 0"
Seating capacity	50
Length of seats	36"
Width of aisle	20"
Weight of car body	24,000 lbs.
Weight of trucks	15,000 lbs.

BOTTOM FRAME. Two outside sills of 4½" x 7¾" and 1¾" x 6" yellow pine with ⅝" x 7¾" steel plate bolted between. Two center sills of 6" steel I-beams filled with yellow pine. Two intermediate sills of 3" x 6" yellow pine; ¾" tie rods with turn-buckles in center at each cross sill. Longitudinal sills are supported on and bolted to two 6" steel I needle beams, two 8" steel plate bolsters and two ¾" x 6" end sill plates.

TRUSSES. Two under truss rods 1⅜" diameter on malleable iron brackets for needle beams. Two inside truss bars ½" x 2" on pedestals over bolsters for supporting overhanging ends.

FLOOR. Of ⅞" x 3¼" yellow pine thoroughly painted on both sides.

BODY. Pullman type windows with steam coach style of framing with alternate single and panel posts, and with ¾" x 2" vertical sheathing on outside.

ROOF. Monitor deck style with steam coach hoods covered with No. 8 canvas, concealed steel rafter at each panel post.

VESTIBULES. At each end with floor 5½" below car floor, with double steps, trap doors and single swing door on each side. Six sills reinforced with ½" x 5" steel plates under each platform.

TOILET ROOM. In one corner of car with dry hopper, cement floor, white enamel finish and water cooler in alcove on outside.

WINDOWS. Twin style with Gothic head; fitted with Edwards' sash fixtures and Pantasote curtains on spring rollers. Deck sashes hung on Harts' ratchets.

DOORS. 30" sliding door in each end bulkhead.

GLASS. D. T. A. selected car glass in all lower window, door and bulkhead sashes, cathedral art glass in zinc channels in Gothic and deck sashes.

INTERIOR FINISH. Quarter-sawed oak, monitor deck ceiling with three-ply quartered oak veneer and bronze trimmings.

SEATS. Hale & Kilburn's No. 99-A type with 19" reversible backs, grab handle and upholstered in white woven rattan.

GRAB HANDLES. Of hickory, in malleable iron sockets on each corner and vestibule post; also diagonal handle on outside of each side door.

WINDOW GUARDS. Bronze on end windows and four-rod painted iron guards on outside of side windows, hinged at tops for cleaning glass.

LIGHTING. Material for 20 lamps on separate bases and couplings at each end for motor car light circuit, are supplied and installed by Car Builder.

DRAW BARS AND COUPLERS. Should be similar to Purchaser's motor car equipment. Supplied and attached by Purchaser at destination, or by Car Builder at extra cost of same.

HEATERS. Supplied and installed by Purchaser, or by Car Builder at extra cost of same.

HAND BRAKES. Malleable iron Lindstrom lever on each end of car.

MISCELLANEOUS FITTINGS. Signal bells and emergency tools are supplied by Car Builder.

AIR BRAKES. Supplied and installed by Purchaser at destination or by Car Builder at extra charge for same.

TRUCKS. Baldwin Class 60-22-T with 33", 550 lbs. chilled cast iron wheels with 3½" treads, on 4⅛" trailer axles, with 4¼" x 8" journals, are supplied by Car Builder and attached to car by Purchaser at destination.

Price can be quoted on duplicates of this car as specified above, or state exceptions desired.

Detail specifications and drawings are submitted for Purchaser's approval before starting work.

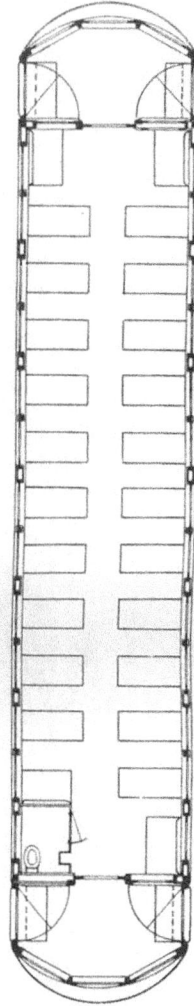

Drawing No. 377—Plan of "Double End" Single Compartment Interurban Trailer Car

Engraving No. 421—"Double End" Interurban Passenger and Smoking Car

48 FT. "DOUBLE END" INTERURBAN PASSENGER CAR

With smoking compartment, toilet room, hot water heater in one vestibule and switch cabinet in the other, and passenger entrance at curb side of rear end and devil strip side of front end when running with either end forward.

For railways having steep or long grades, or on which light, strong cars for fast speed and quick acceleration are desirable, and where most of the loading and discharging of passengers is done at terminal stations and with few stops for local traffic, this plan is recommended.

General Specifications

Length over buffers	48′ 0″	Distance between bolster centers	25′ 6″
Length over vestibules	46′ 8″	Wheel base of trucks	6′ 6″
Length of car body	37′ 1″	Seating capacity	50
Length of vestibules	4′ 9½″	Length of seats	37″
Width at sills, including sheathing	8′ 7½″	Width of aisle	20½″
Width over all	8′ 10″	Weight of car body	26,000 lbs.
Height, under sills to top of roof	9′ 5″	Weight of trucks	17,940 lbs.
Height, track to top of roof	12′ 8″		

Bottom Frame. Double outside sills of 4½″ x 7¾″ and 1¾″ x 6″ yellow pine with ⅝″ x 7¾″ steel plate bolted between. Four center and intermediate sills of 6″ steel I-beams filled with yellow pine, extending under vestibules from buffer to buffer and supported on and bolted to 6″ I needle beams and 10″ plate bolsters; ¾″ tie rods with turnbuckles in center at each cross sill. Sills are spaced to accommodate G. E. 1200 V.—D. C. apparatus.

Trusses. Under truss rods 1½″ diameter; inside truss bars ½″ x 2″ for supporting overhanging ends.

Floor. Double, of ⅞″ x 3¼″ yellow pine with waterproof building felt between, and covered with Greenwich inlaid linoleum.

Body. Steam coach style with twin Gothic windows and sheathed outside with ¾″ x 2″ poplar.

Roof. Monitor deck style with steam coach hoods, covered with No. 8 canvas and fitted with trolley platform whole length.

Vestibules. At each end with 30″ swing door, triple steps and trap doors at curb side of rear end and opposite side of front end. A switch cabinet is located in one vestibule and hot water heater in the other at sides opposite from steps.

Smoking Room. At one end of car occupying the length of four side windows, with swing door and Blount door check in partition.

Toilet Room. In one corner, with dry hopper, cement floor, white enamel finish and water cooler in alcove on outside.

Windows. Pullman style with Edwards' sash fixtures, Pantasote curtains and Forsyth curtain fixtures. Deck sashes hinged at ends and operated by double bronze sash openers.

Doors. 30″ sliding doors in end bulkheads. All other doors of single swing type.

Glass. Heavy polished plate glass in all doors. D. T. A. selected car glass in all lower windows and bulkheads; opalescent rippled glass in zinc channels in Gothic sashes and small panes in deck sashes.

Interior Finish. Selected mahogany with high piers on panel posts, semi-empire ceiling in green and gold. Twelve bronze parcel racks with rod bottoms and bronze trimmings.

Seats. Hale & Kilburn's No. 99-EE type with 26″ back, bronze grab handles, spring edge, upholstered with plush in main compartment and leather in smoking room.

Grab Handles. Hickory, in malleable iron sockets at each side of vestibule doors.

Window Guards. Bronze on end and bulkhead windows. No outside guards.

Lighting. Material for 30 lamps on separate bases on arches of ceiling and wiring for headlight, are supplied and installed by Car Builder. Purchaser inserts lamps at destination.

Draw Bars and Couplers. Janney radial automatic M. C. B. style.

Track Sanders. One Nichols-Lintern air sander with emergency valve on each end of car.

Pilot. One locomotive style under each end of car, located so as not to prevent coupling.

Trolley Retriever. One Knutson No. 2 on each end of car.

Heater. Smith No. 2-C hot water type located in one vestibule.

Switch Cabinet. Asbestos lined, with hinged door, at right-hand side of one vestibule.

Hand Brakes. With Lindstrom lever, in each vestibule.

Miscellaneous Fittings. Signal bells, alarm gongs, switch iron, emergency tools, roof steps, mats and handles, are supplied by Car Builder. Fare registers, headlights, rear lamps and power cable, are supplied by Purchaser.

Air Brakes. Supplied and installed by Purchaser at destination.

Electric Power Equipment. Supplied and installed by Purchaser at destination.

Trucks. Baldwin Class 78-25-A with Standard rolled steel wheels on 5½″ steel axles with 4¼″ x 8″ journals and prepared for General Electric No. 205 100 H. P. motors, are supplied by Car Builder and attached by Purchaser at destination. If cars can be delivered on their own wheels, the trucks should be attached at car works.

Price can be quoted on duplicates of car as specified above, or state exceptions desired. Detail specifications and drawings are prepared for Purchaser's approval before starting work.

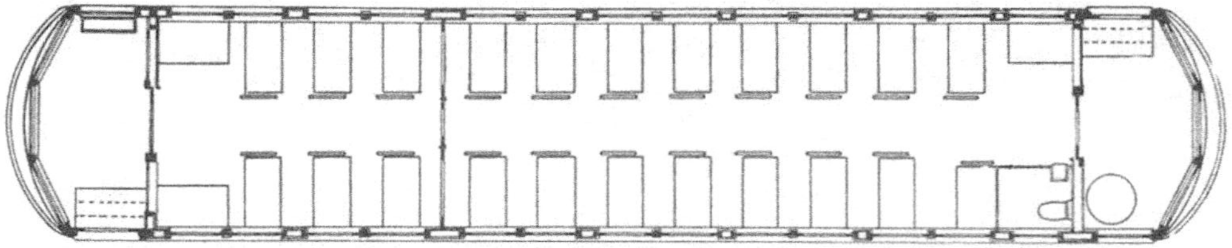

Drawing No. 421—Plan of "Double End" Interurban Passenger and Smoking Car

Engraving No. 388—"Double End" One Compartment Suburban Car

SUBURBAN AND LIGHT INTERURBAN CAR

Suitable for short interurban lines and distant suburbs where a maximum speed of 30 to 35 miles per hour is sufficient and a toilet room is not necessary; for running with either end forward; for either longitudinal or cross seats with center aisle; and at the same time suited to city service over short curves, for frequent stops and quick loading and discharge of passengers. This is a light, cheap car of large carrying capacity for its weight.

General Specifications

Length of car body over end plates	30' 0"
Length of vestibules	4' 10"
Length over vestibules	39' 8"
Length over buffers	41' 0"
Width at sills, including panels	8' 2½"
Width over all	8' 5"
Height, under sills to top of roof	9' 0"
Height, track to top of roof	12' 1"
Distance between bolster centers	19' 0"
Wheel base of trucks	4' 7"
Seating capacity	44
Length of seats	33¾"
Width of aisle	21"
Weight of car body	about 16,000 lbs.
Weight of suitable trucks (two per car)	12,000 lbs.

BOTTOM FRAME. Each of the two outside sills are of one piece of yellow pine, 4½" x 7¾", one piece 1¾" x 6", with a steel plate ⅜" x 7¾" securely bolted between, full length of car body. Two center sills are 3" x 6" yellow pine; ¾" tie rod with turnbuckle in center full width of car at each cross sill.

FLOOR. Double thickness of ⅞" x 3¼" yellow pine with waterproof building felt between and with trap doors over motors.

TRUSSES. Two under truss rods of suitable size, supporting two 6" steel I needle beams and two inside truss bars ⅜" x 2½".

VESTIBULES. Depressed 6" below car floor, with double steps, folding doors and hickory grab handles on each side, three sashes in ends and sheathed outside with No. 14 sheet steel.

BODY. Has single side posts with concealed ½" rods full height, vertical sheathing ¾" x 2", double sash windows, the upper ones stationary and lower ones to raise and all glazed with double strength car glass. 30" sliding door in each end.

ROOF. Of monitor deck style with steam coach hood, concealed steel rafters at each post, eleven ventilator sashes on Hart's ratchet fixtures on each side, covered with No. 8 duck thoroughly painted and fitted with trolley board full length.

INTERIOR FINISH. Of quarter-sawed oak with oak veneer ceiling.

CURTAINS. Of Pantasote, on spring roller fixtures.

SEATS. Eighteen Hale & Kilburn's No. 99-A rattan spring cross seats and backs with bronze grab handles and four longitudinal corner seats.

LIGHTING. Wire and sockets for 20 lamps on separate bases, fuses and switches supplied and installed by Car Builder.

DRAW BARS. Niles radial spring style with Hovey type of coupler, on each end of car.

TRACK SANDERS. One Nichols-Lintern air style on each end of car.

FENDERS. One Berg style on each end of car.

HEADLIGHT. One Mosher arc style with brackets on each vestibule.

TROLLEY CATCHER. Attached by Car Builder if supplied by Purchaser.

REGISTER AND FIXTURES. Attached by Car Builder if supplied by Purchaser.

HEATER. One Smith No. 2-B hot water heater and one corner seat to be removable and occupy same location in different seasons.

HAND BRAKES. In each vestibule, bronze ratchet handle with Peacock C drum.

AIR BRAKES. Are supplied by Purchaser and may be installed by Car Builder at shop cost plus 10%.

ELECTRIC POWER EQUIPMENT. Is supplied and installed by Purchaser at destination or installation may be made by Car Builder at shop cost plus 10%.

TRUCKS. Are supplied and attached by Purchaser at destination or by Car Builder at extra cost for same.

WHEELS. 33" cast iron; 450 pounds; 3" tread; 1" flange.

AXLES. Hammered steel: A. S. & I. R. A. Standard E. A., 4½" diameter at center.

If price is wanted on this car, state that it is to be as specified above or name exceptions desired.

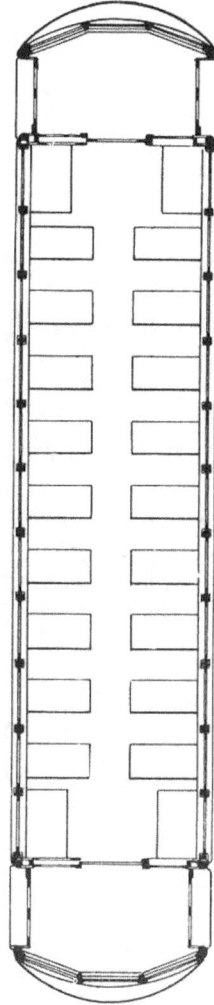

Drawing No. 388—Plan of "Double End" One Compartment Suburban Car

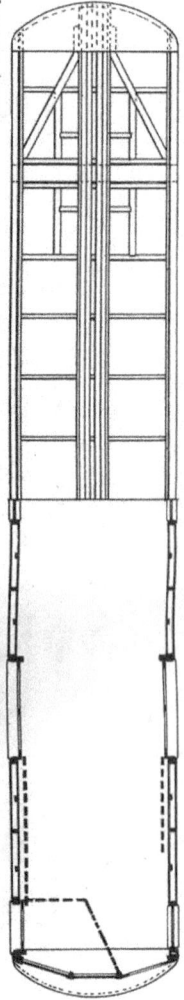

Engraving No. 420—Arch Roof "Double End" Express. Baggage and Freight Car

52 FT. "DOUBLE END" EXPRESS, BAGGAGE AND FREIGHT CAR

having single arch roof, two 5 ft. sliding doors for freight and door for motorman on each side, also swing door in each end for handling long articles.

This style of roof allows high doors, (7 ft. high, 5 ft. wide) so bulky articles, horses, etc. can be loaded. The motorman is enclosed and protected from freight at each end by heavy stanchions and has doors to both outside and inside of car.

These cars also are used for general utility, switching, construction work, snow plows, etc., and are made of any length desired.

GENERAL SPECIFICATIONS:

Length over buffers	52' 0"
Length over vestibules	50' 4"
Length inside between motorman's cabs for freight	41' 8"
Width, extreme, about	8' 7½"
Width over outside sill channels	8' 5"
Width inside between sheathing for freight	7' 7½"
Height under side of sills to top of roof	9' 6"
Height from rails to top of roof with 34" wheels	12' 9"
Distance between bolster centers	34' 0"
Wheel base of trucks	6' 6"
Weight of car body without load, approximate	24,000 lbs.
Weight of trucks, approximate	18,000 lbs.

BOTTOM FRAME: Two outside sills are of 5" x 8" yellow pine, reinforced with 8" steel channel bolted to outside. Two center sills of 6" steel I beams filled with yellow pine, and are supported on and bolted to 6 transverse steel beams, viz: two 8" needle I beams, two steel plate bolsters and two steel channels under end sills. Tie rods ¾" with turnbuckle in center at each cross sill.

TRUSSES: Two under truss rods of 1½" round steel supporting two 8" steel I needle beams.

FLOOR: Of 2" tongue and groove oak planks crosswise, thoroughly painted on both sides.

BODY: Posts of oak with ½" vertical rods, plates of yellow pine, outside sheathing of ¾" poplar, inside of ⅞" yellow pine or ash; bracing similar to steam car practice.

ROOF: Of single arch style full length over vestibules, reinforced with 10 steel carlines, roof boards ½" covered with No. 8 canvas, painted and fitted with trolley plank full length.

VESTIBULES: At each end having two sashes and 30" swinging door in end, sash in left side and door in right side for motorman. Vertical stanchions from floor to roof with 20" swinging door at each end of car to separate motorman from freight.

WIRING: and fixtures for light and power supplied and installed by purchaser at destination.

COUPLERS AND DRAW BARS: Face of each buffer fitted with heavy steel draw head, securely bolted to steel center sills and a 6 ft. coupling bar 3" x 1½" carried on hooks under side of car. Radial couplers to fit Purchaser's standard equipment or automatic M. C. B. radial draw bars to couple with steam railroad cars may be fitted to under sides of buffers at extra cost of same.

TRACK SANDERS: One compressed air sander on each end of car arranged to drop sand under leading wheels.

PILOTS OR FENDERS: Supplied and attached by Purchaser at destination.

HEADLIGHTS: Supplied and attached by Purchaser at destination.

TROLLEY RETRIEVER: Supplied and attached by Purchaser at destination.

HEATER: Supplied and attached by Purchaser at destination.

HAND BRAKES: On each end of car with vertical geared iron wheel.

MISCELLANEOUS FITTINGS: 2 alarm gongs, 2 signal bells with cord, 2 switch irons, 2 sets of roof steps, grab handles and iron stirrup steps at each door, and socket in each corner of car for tail lamps and flags, are supplied by Car Builder.

AIR BRAKES: Supplied and installed by Purchaser at destination or may be installed by Car Builder at shop cost plus 10 per cent.

ELECTRIC POWER EQUIPMENT: Supplied and installed by Purchaser at destination, or may be installed by Car Builder at shop cost plus 10 per cent.

TRUCKS: Baldwin Class 78-30-A with 34" rolled steel wheels on 5½" hammered steel axles with 4¼" x 8" journals, are suitable for this car. If cars can be delivered on track on their own wheels, it is advisable to have trucks supplied and fitted by Car Builder at Car Works, otherwise by Purchaser at destination.

If price is wanted on this car, state that it is to be as specified above and name exceptions desired. Detail drawings and specifications are submitted for purchaser's approval before starting work.

Drawing No. 420—Plan of "Double End" Express, Baggage and Freight Car

Engraving No. 258 Monitor Roof "Single End" Express Baggage and Freight Car

45 FT. "SINGLE END" EXPRESS, BAGGAGE AND FREIGHT CAR having monitor deck roof, one 6 ft. sliding door for freight and swinging door for employees on each side, also swinging door in end of rear vestibule for handling long material.

This style of car is made of any length desired by Purchaser and has proven one of the most convenient and satisfactory types on many electric railways.

GENERAL SPECIFICATIONS:

Length over buffers	44' 10"
Length over vestibules	43' 2"
Length inside between end bulkheads or stanchions for freight	35' 3"
Width, extreme, about	8' 4"
Width, over outside sheathing at sills	8' 1½"
Width, inside between sheathing for freight	7' 4"
Height, under side of sills to top of roof	9' 4"
Height, from rails to top of roof with 33" wheels	12' 6"
Distance between bolster centers	25' 7½"
Wheel base of trucks	6' 6"
Weight of car body, without load, approximate	21,500 lbs.
Weight of trucks, approximate	16,500 lbs.

BOTTOM FRAME: Two outside sills built up of 4½" x 7¾" and 13¼" x 6" yellow pine with 5/8"x7¾" steel plate bolted between; two center sills of 6" steel I beams filled with yellow pine and two intermediate sills of 3½" x 6" yellow pine. Tie rods ¾" with turnbuckle in center at each cross sill.

TRUSSES: Two under truss rods of 1¼" round steel supporting two 6" steel needle I beams.

FLOOR: Of 1¾" tongue and groove hard maple or oak planks.

BODY: Posts of oak or ash with ½" vertical rods, plates and deck sills of yellow pine, outside sheathing of ¾" poplar, inside of ⅞" yellow pine, bracing similar to steam car practice.

ROOF: Reinforced with 11 steel rafters, 12 deck sashes on each side, one half of which are movable, ½" roof boards covered with No. 8 canvas and painted.

VESTIBULES: Front with 3 sashes across end, 1 at left side and swinging door at right side; rear with 2 sashes and swinging door in end, sash in left side and swinging door in right side. Each vestibule is separated from freight by 2" iron pipe vertical stanchions from floor to end plate with 24" opening at left hand side.

WIRING: With keyless sockets for 10 lamps along ceiling, for headlight at each end, and concealed portion of power cable by Car Builder. Purchaser to insert lamps at destination.

COUPLERS AND DRAW BARS: Face of each buffer fitted with heavy steel draw-head securely bolted to steel center sills and a 6 ft. coupling bar 3" x 1½" carried on hooks under side of car. Automatic M. C. B. radial draw bars and couplers also may be fitted to under sides of buffers at extra cost of same.

TRACK SANDERS: On front end of car, arranged to drop sand under leading wheels on both rails.

PILOT: One locomotive style under front end of car and not to extend beyond buffers.

HEADLIGHT: Supplied by Purchaser, wiring and brackets for same supplied and attached by Car Builder.

TROLLEY RETRIEVER: On rear end of car, supplied and attached by Car Builder.

HEATER: Supplied and installed by Purchaser at destination.

HAND BRAKES, in front vestibule with 12" malleable iron ratchet handle.

MISCELLANEOUS FITTINGS: Alarm gongs, signal bells, rear lamps and flags with corner brackets, switch iron, and desk with pigeon holes are supplied by Car Builder.

AIR BRAKES: Supplied and installed by Purchaser at destination, or may be installed by Car Builder at shop cost plus 10 per cent.

ELECTRIC POWER EQUIPMENT: Supplied and installed by Purchaser at destination, or may be installed by Car Builder at shop cost plus 10 per cent.

TRUCKS: Baldwin Class 78-25-A with 33" rolled steel wheels on 5" hammered steel axles, with 4½" x 8" journals, are suitable for this car. If cars can be delivered on track on their own wheels, it is advisable to have trucks supplied and fitted by Car Builder at Car Works, otherwise by Purchaser at destination.

If price is wanted on this car, state that it is to be as specified above and name exceptions desired.

Detail drawings and specifications are submitted for purchaser's approval before starting work.

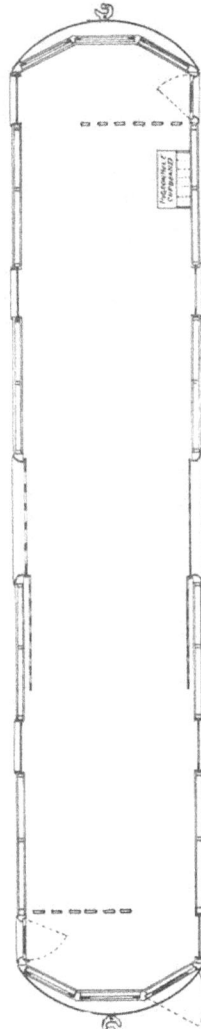

Drawing No. 258 Plan of "Single End" Express, Baggage and Freight Car

Engraving No. 211—Monitor Roof "Double End" Express, Baggage and Freight Car

51 FT. "DOUBLE END" EXPRESS, BAGGAGE AND FREIGHT CAR having monitor deck roof, two 6-ft. sliding doors for freight on each side, swinging door in one end for loading long material and motorman's door at right side of each vestibule.

This car is made to resemble passenger cars as much as possible, and is preferable to the single-arch roof type for use on city streets where appearance is important.

The rapidly increasing express and package freight business of interurban railways makes these cars very profitable and convenient to both owners and shippers.

GENERAL SPECIFICATIONS:

Length over buffers	51' 0"
Length over vestibules	49' 4"
Length inside between end stanchions for freight	41' 2"
Width, extreme, about	8' 6"
Width over outside sheathing at sills	8' 3½"
Width inside between sheathing for freight	7' 6"
Height, under side of sills to top of roof	9' 4"
Height from rails to top of roof with 34" wheels	12' 7"
Distance between truck centers	30' 0"
Wheel base of trucks	6' 6"
Weight of car body without load, approximate	24,000 lbs.
Weight of trucks, approximate	18,000 lbs.

BOTTOM FRAME: Two outside sills of 4½" x 7¾" and 1¾" x 6" yellow pine, with ⅝" x 7¾" steel plate bolted between; two center sills of 6" steel I beams filled with yellow pine and two intermediate sills of 3½" x 6" yellow pine. The six longitudinal sills are supported on and bolted to six transverse steel beams, viz: two needle beams, two bolsters and two steel channels under end sills. Tie rods, ¾" with turnbuckle in center at each cross sill.

TRUSSES: Two under truss rods of 1½" round steel supporting two 8" steel needle I beams.

FLOOR: Of 1¾" tongue and groove hard maple or oak planks.

BODY: Posts of oak or ash, with ½" vertical rods, plates and deck sills of yellow pine, outside sheathing of ¾" poplar, inside of ⅞" yellow pine, bracing similar to steam car practice.

ROOF: Reinforced with thirteen steel carlines, fourteen deck sashes on each side, one-half of which are movable, ½" roof boards covered with No. 8 canvas and painted.

VESTIBULES: Front with three sashes in end, one in left side and swinging door in right side; rear with two sashes and swinging door in end, one sash in left side and swinging door in right side. Each vestibule is separated from freight by 2" iron pipe vertical stanchions from floor to end plate with 24" opening at left hand side.

WIRING: With keyless sockets for fifteen lamps along center of ceiling, for headlight at each end, and concealed portion of power cable by Car Builder. Purchaser to insert lamps at destination.

COUPLERS AND DRAW BARS: Face of each buffer fitted with heavy steel draw head, securely bolted to steel center sills and a 6-ft. coupling bar, 3" x 1½", carried on hooks under side of car. Automatic M. C. B. radial draw bars and couplers also may be fitted to under sides of buffers at extra cost of same.

TRACK SANDERS: Of compressed air style on each end of car, arranged to drop sand under leading wheels on both rails.

PILOT: One locomotive style under each end of car, and not to extend beyond buffers, so as to allow coupling to other cars.

HEADLIGHT: Supplied by Purchaser, wiring and brackets for same supplied and attached by Car Builder.

TROLLEY RETRIEVER: On each end of car, supplied and attached by Car Builder.

HEATER: Supplied and installed by Purchaser at destination.

HAND BRAKES: In each vestibule with 12' malleable iron ratchet handle.

MISCELLANEOUS FITTINGS: Alarm gongs, signal bells, rear lamps and flags with corner brackets, switch iron, and desk with pigeon holes are supplied by Car Builder.

AIR BRAKES: Supplied and installed by Purchaser at destination, or may be installed by Car Builder at shop cost plus ten per cent.

ELECTRIC POWER EQUIPMENT: Supplied and installed by Purchaser at destination, or may be installed by Car Builder at shop cost plus ten per cent.

TRUCKS: Baldwin class, 78-30-A, with 34" rolled steel wheels on 5½" hammered steel axles, with 4¼" x 8" journals, are suitable for this car. If cars can be delivered on track on their own wheels, it is advisable to have trucks supplied and fitted by Car Builder at Car Works, otherwise by Purchaser at destination.

If price is wanted on this car, state that it is to be as specified above and name exceptions desired.

Detail drawings and specifications are submitted for purchaser's approval before starting work.

Drawing No. 211—Plan of "Double End" Express, Baggage and Freight Car

45 FT. "DOUBLE END" EXPRESS, BAGGAGE AND FREIGHT CAR having single arch roof, 6-ft. sliding door for freight and swinging door for employees on each side and swinging door for loading long material in each end.

For roads on which it is not essential that the express cars resemble passenger cars, the arch roof style is equally as good as the monitor deck, as it permits higher doors and is cheaper

When fitted with M. C. B. couplers and rigid draw heads on buffers with 6-ft. coupling link, the car can be used for switching all other kinds of cars.

Removable snow plows can be attached for winter service and the car is valuable for repair and general construction work.

We build cars of this type of any length desired by purchaser.

GENERAL SPECIFICATIONS:

Length over buffers	45' 0"
Length over vestibules	43' 1"
Length inside between end stanchions for freight	35' 1½"
Width, extreme, about	8' 8"
Width over outside sheathing at sills	8' 5½"
Height inside between sheathing for freight	7' 8"
Height under side of sills to top of roof	9' 4"
Height from rails to top of roof with 33" wheels	12' 4¾"
Distance between bolster centers	25' 0"
Wheel base of trucks	6' 6"
Weight of car body without load, approximate	21,000 lbs.
Weight of trucks, approximate	16,500 lbs.

BOTTOM FRAME: Two outside sills of yellow pine, 5" x 8", with ¾" x 7" steel plate bolted to outside. Two center sills of 6" steel I beams filled with yellow pine. Tie rods, ¾", with turnbuckle in center at each cross sill.

TRUSSES: Two under truss rods of 1¼" round steel supporting two 6" steel needle I beams.

FLOOR: Of 1¾" tongue and groove hard maple or oak planks.

BODY: Posts of oak or ash with ½" vertical rods, plates and deck sills of yellow pine, outside sheathing of ¾" poplar, inside of ⅞" yellow pine, bracing similar to steam car practice.

ROOF: Of single arch style full length over vestibules, reinforced with steel carlines, ½" roof boards covered with No. 8 canvas, painted, fitted with trolley plank full length and roof mats.

VESTIBULES: Two sashes and swinging door in each car end, one sash on left side and swinging door on right side. Each vestibule is separated from freight by 2" iron pipe vertical stanchions from floor to end plates with 24" opening at left hand side.

WIRING: With keyless sockets for ten lamps along ceiling, for headlight at each end, and concealed portion of power cable by Car Builder, Purchaser to insert lamps at destination.

COUPLERS AND DRAW BARS: Face of each buffer fitted with heavy steel draw head, securely bolted to steel center sills and a 6 ft. coupling bar, 3" x 1½", carried on hooks under side of draw. Radial couplers to fit purchaser's standard equipment or automatic M. C. B. radial draw bars to couple with steam railroad cars may be fitted to under sides of buffers at extra cost of same.

Engraving No. 365—Arch Roof "Double End" Express, Baggage and Freight Car

TRACK SANDERS: One compressed air sander on each end of car arranged to drop sand under leading wheels.

PILOTS OR FENDERS: Supplied and attached by Purchaser at destination.

HEADLIGHT: Supplied by Purchaser; wiring and brackets for same supplied and attached to each vestibule by Car Builder.

TROLLEY RETRIEVERS: To be supplied and attached by Purchaser at destination.

HEATER: One large cast-iron stove for burning hard or soft coal, located in one corner of car and protected from freight by iron bars.

HAND BRAKES: In each vestibule, fitted with 12" malleable-iron ratchet handle.

MISCELLANEOUS FITTINGS: Two alarm gongs, two signal bells, two switch irons, two colored signal lamps and flags with sockets on each corner of car, trolley hook at each end of roof and grab handles and iron stirrup steps at each door, are supplied by Car Builder.

AIR BRAKES: Supplied and installed by Purchaser at destination or may be installed by Car Builder at shop cost plus ten per cent.

ELECTRIC POWER EQUIPMENT: Supplied and installed by Purchaser at destination, or may be installed by Car Builder at shop cost plus ten per cent.

TRUCKS: Baldwin class, 78-25-A, with 33" rolled steel wheels on 5" hammered steel axles, with 4¼" x 8" journals, are suitable for this car. If cars can be delivered on track on their own wheels, it is advisable to have trucks supplied and fitted by Car Builder at Car Works, otherwise by Purchaser at destination.

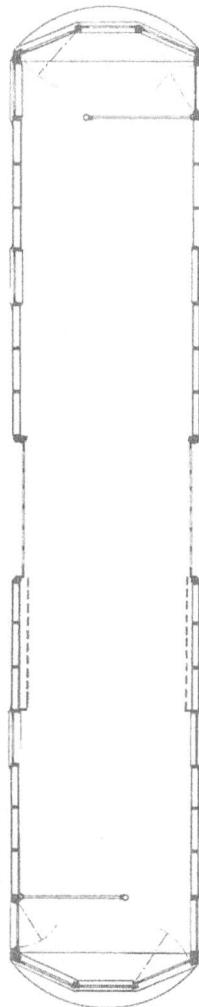

If price is wanted on this car, state that it is to be as specified above, and name exceptions desired.
Detail drawings and specifications are submitted for purchaser's approval before starting work.

Drawing No. 365—Plan of "Double End" Express, Baggage and Freight Car

SOME WELL KNOWN NILES CARS WITH GOOD SEATING PLANS

Car No. 370

Car No. 340

Car No. 363

Car No. 286

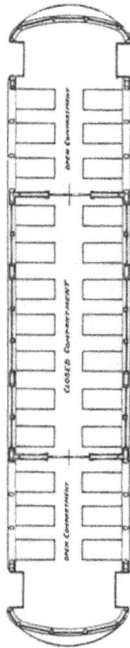

46 Ft. "Double End" California Type Open and Closed Car

Length over buffers	45' 10"
Length of body	35' 6"
Length of closed compartment	18' 4"
Seating capacity	52 persons

Weight of body, about........24,000 lbs.
Weight complete on track with four 50 H. P.
600 V. D. C. motors about........26 tons

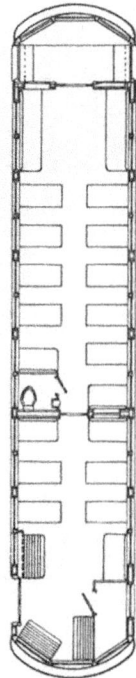

46 Ft. "Single End" Combination Passenger, Smoking and Baggage Car

Length over buffers	46' 4"
Length of body	34' 0"
Length of passenger compartment	22' 11"
Length of smoking-baggage room	16' 11"

Seating capacity........48 persons
Weight of body, about........24,500 lbs.
Weight complete on track with four 50 H. P.
600 V. D. C. motors, about........27 tons

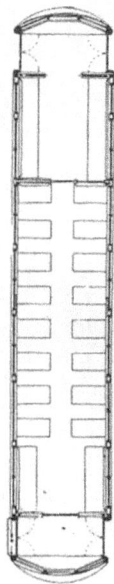

48 Ft. "Double End" Two Compartment Passenger and Smoking Car

Length over buffers	47' 8"
Length of body	37' 0"
Length of passenger compartment	27' 10¾"
Seating capacity	48 persons

Weight of body, about........25,000 lbs.
Weight complete on track with four 50 H. P.
600 V. D. C. motors, about........26½ tons

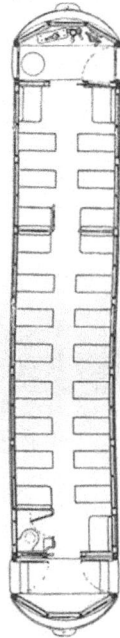

49 Ft. "Single End" Two Compartment Passenger and Smoking Car

Length over buffers	49' 0"
Length of body	37' 1½"
Length of passenger compartment	25' 10¾"
Seating capacity	50 persons

Weight of body, about........26,000 lbs.
Weight complete on track with four 75 H.P.
600 V. D. C. motors, about........30 tons

SOME WELL KNOWN NILES CARS WITH GOOD SEATING PLANS

50 Ft. "Single End" Three Compartment, Passenger, Smoking and Baggage Car

Length over buffers .... 50' 4"
Length of body .... 40' 2"
Length of passenger compartment .... 28' 1"
Length of smoking room .... 8' 2"
Toilet on rear platform

Seating capacity .... 52 persons
Weight of body, about .... 27,500 lbs
Weight complete on track with four 75 H.P.
600 V.D.C. motors, about .... 31 tons

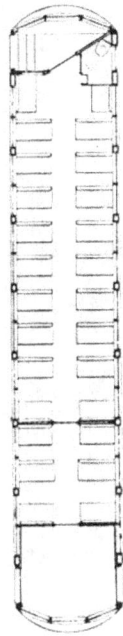

50 Ft. "Single End" Three Compartment, Passenger, Smoking and Baggage Car

Length over buffers .... 50' 4"
Length of body .... 39' 8½"
Length of passenger compartment .... 22' 8"
Length of smoking room .... 10' 10½"
Seating capacity .... 46 persons

Baggage capacity
Weight of car body, about .... 2,000 lbs
Weight complete on track with four 75 H.P.
1,200 V.D.C. motors, about .... 38 tons

51 Ft. "Single End" Two Compartment, Passenger and Smoking Car

Length over buffers .... 51' 10"
Length of body .... 40' 0"
Seating capacity .... 54 persons

Weight of body, about .... 27,000 lbs
Weight complete on track with four 60 H.P.
600 V.D.C. motors, about .... 30½ tons

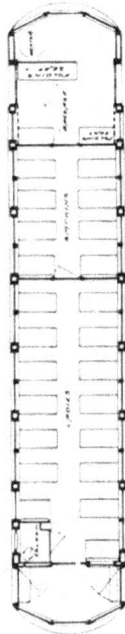

51 Ft. "Single End" Three Compartment, Passsenger, Smoking and Baggage Car

Length over buffers .... 51' 0"
Length of passenger compartment .... 22' 9"
Length of baggage vestibule .... 11' 0"
Seating capacity .... 45 persons

Baggage capacity, about
Weight of car body, about .... 2,000 lbs
Weight complete on track with four 75 H.P.
600 V.D.C. motors, about .... 30½ tons

Car No. 306

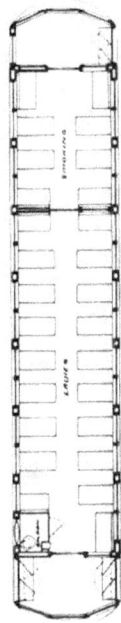

Car No. 324

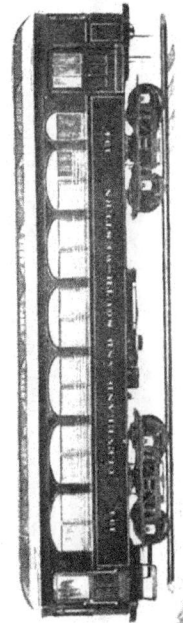

Car No. 198

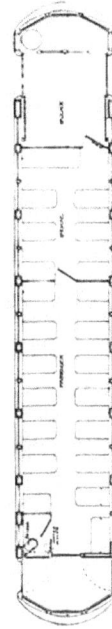

Car No. 201

SOME WELL KNOWN NILES CARS WITH GOOD SEATING PLANS

Car No. 278

Car No. 238

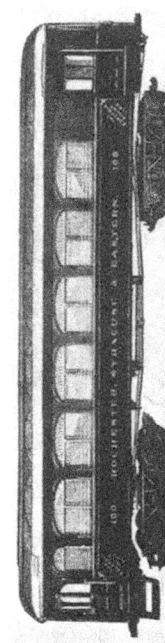

Car No. 208

Car No. 228

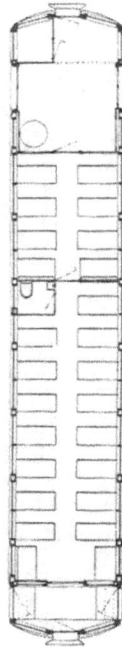

53 Ft. "Single End" Three Compartment, Passenger, Smoking and Baggage Car

Length over buffers .... 53' 3⅝"
Length of body .... 43' 6½"
Length of passenger compartment .... 25' 4"
Seating capacity .... 50 persons

Baggage capacity, about .... 2,000 lbs.
Weight of body, about .... 30,000 lbs.
Weight complete on track with four 75 H. P.
600 V. D. C. motors, about .... 34 tons

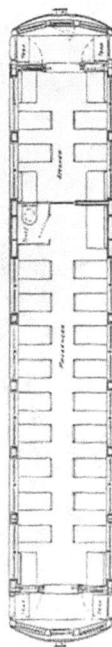

53 Ft. "Double End" Steel Underframe, Passenger and Smoking Car

Length over buffers .... 52' 10½"
Length of body .... 44' 4½"
Length of passenger compartment .... 32' 3¾"
Seating capacity .... 58 persons

Weight of body, about .... 35,000 lbs.
Weight complete on track with four 125 H. P.
600 V. D. C. motors, about .... 40 tons

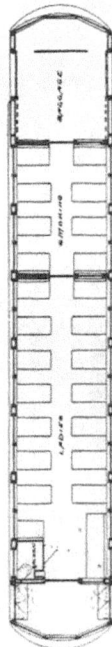

53 Ft. "Single End" Three Compartment, Passenger, Smoking and Baggage Car

Length over buffers .... 53' 6"
Length of body .... 42' 8"
Seating capacity .... 46 persons
Baggage capacity, about .... 2,000 lbs.

Weight of body, about .... 30,000 lbs.
Weight complete on track with four 110 H. P.
600 V. D. C. motors, about .... 35 tons

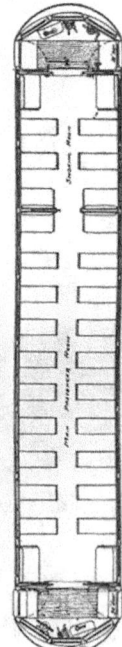

53 Ft. "Double End" Two Compartment, Passenger and Smoking Car

Length over tuffers .... 53' 6"
Length of body .... 42' 8"
Seating capacity .... 60 persons

Weight of body, about .... 29,000 lbs.
Weight complete on track with four 75 H. P.
600 V. D. C. motors, about .... 32 tons

SOME WELL KNOWN NILES CARS WITH GOOD SEATING PLANS

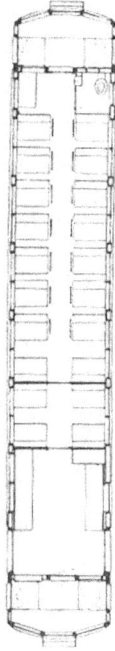

55 Ft. "Double End" Three Compartment, Passenger, Smoking and Baggage Car

Length over buffers .... 55' 0"
Length of body .... 43' 10"
Seating capacity .... 49 persons
Baggage capacity, about .... 2,000 lbs.
Weight of body, about .... 34,000 lbs.
Weight complete on track with four 75 H.P. 1,200 V.D.C. motors, about .... 40 tons

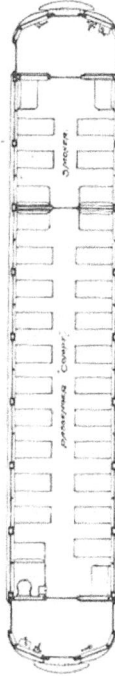

56 Ft. "Double End" Two Compartment, Passenger and Smoking Car

Length over buffers .... 56' 0"
Length of body .... 44' 8"
Seating capacity .... 62 persons
Weight of body, about .... 33,000 lbs.
Weight complete on track with four 100 H.P. A.C. motors, about .... 45 tons

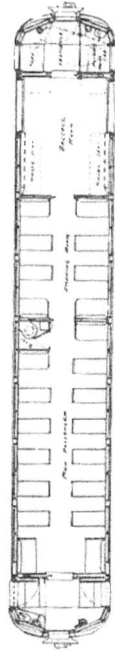

56 Ft. "Double End" Three Compartment, Passenger, Smoking and Baggage Car

Length over buffers .... 56' 0"
Length of body .... 44' 8"
Seating capacity, about .... 56 persons
Baggage capacity, about .... 2,000 lbs.
Weight of body, about .... 32,000 lbs.
Weight complete on track with four 75 H.P. 600 V.D.C. motors, about .... 39 tons

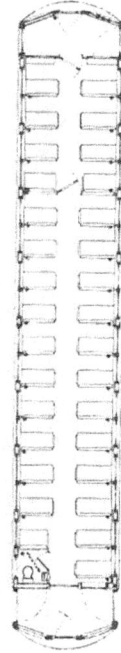

57 Ft. "Single End" Two Compartment, Passenger and Smoking Car

Length over buffers .... 57' 2"
Length of body .... 47' 4"
Seating capacity .... 62 persons
Weight of body, about .... 36,000 lbs.
Weight complete on track with four 125 H.P. A.C. motors, about .... 49 tons

Car No. 331

Car No. 267

Car No. 219

Car No. 343

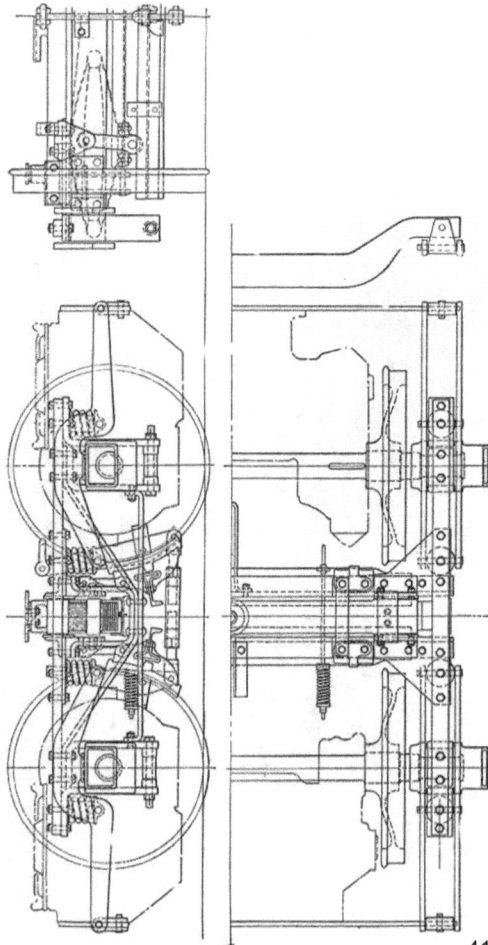

MOTOR TRUCK, CLASS 54-18 F

This is the best and most radical improvement in "short wheel base" trucks for outside hung motors, which are carried on equalizing beams fulcrumed on the journal boxes and spring supported near bolster. Removing the motors from the end frames of the truck permits of lighter frames, springs adjusted for easy riding only, and prevents tilting of truck frame by motors. It is the strongest, lightest, most easy riding, perfectly equalized and most conveniently repaired truck on the market.

Detail specifications of this truck will be supplied upon receipt of motor and car body data.

TRAILER TRUCK, CLASS 60-22 T

This is a light, strong, easy riding trailer truck for interurban cars and fast speed. With depressed end sills and motor supports; it is used as a motor truck for heavy city and suburban service. The truck photographed for engraving at right is in interurban service of the Chicago & Southern Traction Company, while between 2000 and 3000 of this type motor trucks are in city service in Chicago.

41

MOTOR TRUCK, CLASS 78-25 A

This type is the most frequently used under interurban cars, as it is designed for car bodies from 48 ft. to 53 ft. in length, quadruple 60 to 75 H. P. motor equipments and speeds of 40 to 60 miles per hour.

It is fitted with curved equalizing brake bar supported on end sill of truck. Brakes with straight equalizing bar supported on upright brake levers near bolster, as shown in engraving and drawing below, are preferable when clearance of motors and car sills permit, but in most cases where large motors are used and car body carried low the above style of brakes gives better results.

Detail specifications of this truck will be furnished upon receipt of type and H. P. of motors to be used and weight of car body and seating capacity.

MOTOR TRUCK, CLASS 84-30 A

This type is most suitable for interurban cars 55 ft. to 65 ft. in length, quadruple 90 to 125 H. P. motors and speeds of 50 to 70 miles per hour.

The brake equalizing bar is located in center of truck as near the king pin as possible, supported on upper ends of upright levers, the connecting rod extending over the motor. This is preferable where clearances admit, to the brakes surrounding the motor as shown in engraving and drawing at top of page, as it is simpler, reduces friction and not so liable to be torn off when the trucks "split a switch."

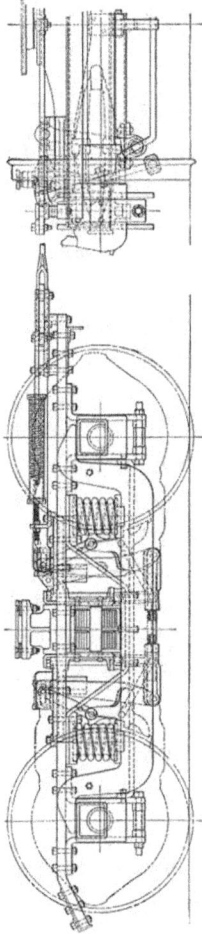

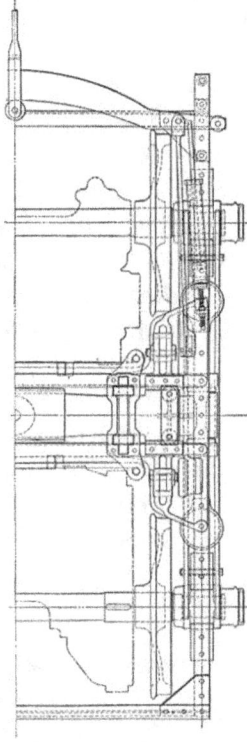

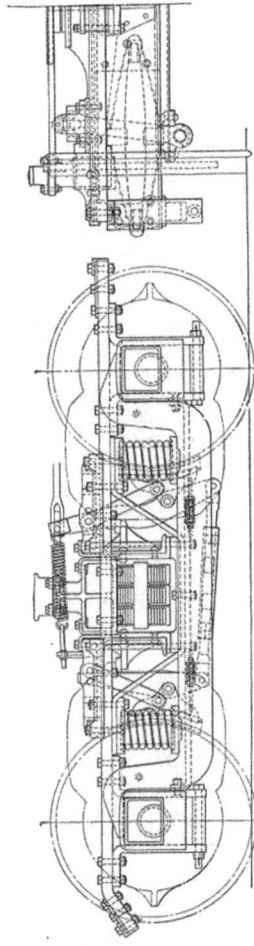

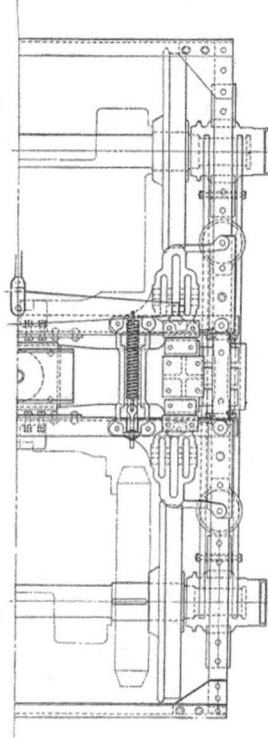

Detail specifications for this truck will be prepared upon receipt of type and horse power of motors to be used, weight of car body and seating capacity.

42

The New York Subway
ITS CONSTRUCTION AND EQUIPMENT

INTERBOROUGH
RAPID
TRANSIT
-1904-

Reprinted by PeriscopeFilm.com

On October 27, 1904, the Interborough Rapid Transit Company opened the first subway in New York City. Running between City Hall and 145th Street at Broadway, the line was greeted with enthusiasm and, in some circles, trepidation. Created under the supervision of Chief Engineer S.L.F. Deyo, the arrival of the IRT foreshadowed the end of the "elevated" transit era on the island of Manhattan. The subway proved such a success that the IRT Co. soon achieved a monopoly on New York public transit. In 1940 the IRT and its rival the BMT were taken over by the City of New York. Today, the IRT subway lines still exist, primarily in Manhattan where they are operated as the "A Division" of the subway. Reprinted here is a special book created by the IRT, recounting the design and construction of the fledgling subway system. Originally created in 1904, it presents the IRT story with a flourish, and with numerous fascinating illustrations and rare photographs.

Originally written in the late 1900's and then periodically revised, A History of the Baldwin Locomotive Works chronicles the origins and growth of one of America's greatest industrial-era corporations. Founded in the early 1830's by Philadelphia jeweler Matthais Baldwin, the company built a huge number of steam locomotives before ceasing production in 1949. These included the 4-4-0 American type, 2-8-2 Mikado and 2-8-0 Consolidation. Hit hard by the loss of the steam engine market, Baldwin soldiered on for a brief while, producing electric and diesel engines. General Electric's dominance of the market proved too much, and Baldwin finally closed its doors in 1956. By that time over 70,500 Baldwin locomotives had been produced. This high quality reprint of the official company history dates from 1920. The book has been slightly reformatted, but care has been taken to preserve the integrity of the text.

NOW AVAILABLE AT
WWW.PERISCOPEFILM.COM

A HISTORY OF THE
BALDWIN
LOCOMOTIVE
WORKS
1831-1920

Reprinted by PeriscopeFilm.com

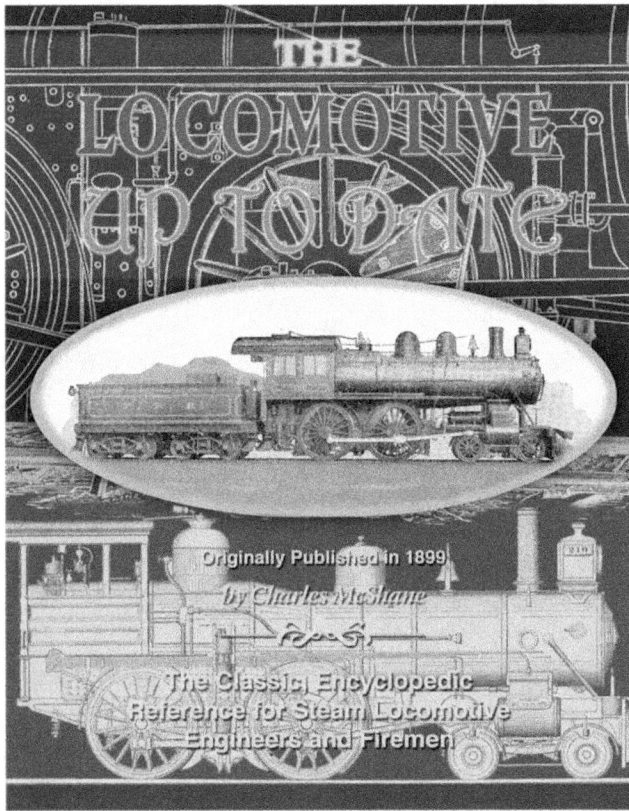